Search
for
Maturity

# Search
# for
# Maturity

by CHARLES C. L. KAO

## THE WESTMINSTER PRESS
Philadelphia

*Book Design by Dorothy Alden Smith*

Published by The Westminster Press
Philadelphia, Pennsylvania

PRINTED IN THE UNITED STATES OF AMERICA

**Library of Congress Cataloging in Publication Data**

Kao, Charles C    L    1932–
    Search for maturity.
    176 p.    21 cm.
    Includes bibliographical references.
    1. Emotional maturity. 2. East and West.
3. Psychology, Religious. I. Title.
BF710.K37                155.2                75–15805
ISBN 0-664-20828-2

# Contents

*(Continued on next page)*

# Preface

ABOUT TEN YEARS AGO, an attractive American girl went to Taiwan in her search for meaning in life. When she became a nun in one of the Buddhist temples in Hsinchu, non-Christians were interested, but Christians were embarrassed. Before long, she became disillusioned and returned to the United States.

There is, today, a widespread interest in Eastern religions especially among young people. Many of them are disgusted with Western traditions, distrustful of societal establishments, and intolerant of the hypocrisies of their leaders. Traditional values, beliefs, and morality are under attack. They are regarded as survivals either of an ancient tribal and superstitious period, or of medieval feudalism, and no longer relevant in a modern scientific technological age. We are all increasingly uncertain about our values, our beliefs, our direction.

The great era of religious expansion in the West has come to an end. Previously unquestioned beliefs are subjected to careful scrutiny; hidden doubts are openly declared as never before. Modern man no longer finds it necessary to depend on Almighty God for support and guidance because problems can be solved scientifically. Religion is no longer required as a frame of reference in comprehending the universe. As one cartoonist well depicts it, people are leaving the sanctuary for the office of a psychiatrist who listens sympathetically. Even the theological tides seem to be moving toward this worldly affirmation.

But in tearing down the old sanctuary, in throwing out mythological hymns and liturgies, and in rejecting oppressive and irrelevant sermons, modern man will do well if he does not destroy the treasure with the earthen vessel. What will be left in the Western heritage after demythologization? When awakened modern minds have grown from childish dependence toward adolescent independence, from tribal magic toward scientific technology, what will be the essence of Christian faith that is still relevant for mature adulthood?

In Asia, there has been a resurgence of interest in Eastern religions. Along with nationalism, this is creating a national cultural consciousness as a self-defense against the invasion of Western ideas. The Buddhists encounter the challenge of modern science and technology in addition to the threat of Communism. Neo-Buddhist scholars in Japan, Burma, and other parts of Southeast Asia seek kinship with the Communist to counterattack Western personal theism. Buddhists of this stream claim that Buddhism is atheism, the most scientific religion of the world, and the forerunner of modern psychoanalysis. Some of its ethical impulses, they insist, are present in Marxism; they say that Buddha was the forerunner of Karl Marx in proclaiming the equality of all men and women. On the mainland of China, traditional Confucianism, Taoism, and Buddhism have been under fire since the People's Republic of China came into being. Traditional ideologies are to be purged by Communism. What would be left in China after this purge? Is the essence of these traditional ideologies still relevant for modern scientific and technological men? What in the past can serve the present and the future?

The "China boom" in the United States has had its ups and downs. But to think of the Chinese only in terms of acupuncture, kung fu, chop suey, and chow mein is utterly inadequate and superficial. The Chinese represent more than these, just as Americans represent more than hamburgers, color televisions, football, and Hollywood. For better relations between the East and the West, deeper understanding of each other's ideological essence, in both the past and the present, is indispensable. Nothing can be more essential for such understanding than the concept of human maturity which reflects man's common aspirations, goals, and objectives. What is maturity? What should be our aspirations, goals, and objectives? Having been born and raised in the East and later exposed to the West, I find myself plagued with these culturally relative questions. Answers to these questions differ from one culture to another.

This book is written for those who are searching for an image of the mature person, of becoming mature, in the context of East-West encounter. It is not intended to be a comparative analysis of the concept of maturity in psychology, Christian theology, Confucianism, Taoism, and Buddhism. Rather it is an effort to synthesize those common factors which constitute the image of an ideal, healthy, mature person in different traditions and from different perspectives. It seeks further to use that ideal for our guidance in this age of uncertainty, bewilderment, and East-West dialogue. The word "maturity" in this book is used in the widest sense, and the word "man," in most cases, is used to signify any human being regardless of sex. The word "harmony" is used in a dynamic sense. The study is based on library research and personal interviews, and is condensed in this form for all, in partial payment of the debt I owe to life.

C. K.

*Brookline, Massachusetts*

# Acknowledgments

AN ACKNOWLEDGMENT of appreciation is due to the many scholars and friends in the greater Boston area and other places who have shared their life experiences and ideas for interviews, have supplied materials related to the study, or have read the manuscript and offered valuable suggestions.

To the following persons and to uncounted others I am indebted: Robert Freed Bales, Kenneth D. Benne, Peter A. Bertocci, Edwin A. Burtt, John B. Carman, Bessie Chambers, Wing-tsit Chan, Robert Chin, Harvey G. Cox, Jr., Paul K. Deats, Jr., A. Deal, Vincent deGregoris, James W. Fowler III, Per Hassing, Y. C. Ho, Richard Hocking, Walter L. Holcomb, William Hung, Merle L. Jordan, Stanley H. King, Lawrence Kohlberg, Y. C. Li, Abraham H. Maslow, T. Scott Miyakawa, W. Clifton Moore, Charles W. Morris, Walter G. Muelder, M. Nagatomi, J. Robert Nelson, Richard R. Niebuhr, Steve C. Pan, Ralph B. Potter, Lucian Pye, William R. Rogers, Jr., Benjamin I. Schwartz, B. F. Skinner, Huston Smith, Wilfred C. Smith, Krister Stendahl, Orlo Strunk, Jr., Robert L. Treese, Ezra F. Vogel, Robert W. White, Preston N. Williams, L. S. Yang.

My most sincere gratitude is also due to the foundation (whose founder wished to do good anonymously) for its grant in support of the continuing project the preliminary stages of which in the form of interviews has enriched the content of this book considerably.

Finally, I am grateful to my wife and son, who have endured the burden with me during the period of study and writing.

# I

## A New Era,
## East and West

A FEW YEARS AGO, the mood of American society was very well described by a news reporter who wrote "Change Is King," [1] and its culture was aptly labeled by a university president as "instant culture." [2] Indeed, we live in an era in which nothing is constant except change itself. This is an era in which man's search for maturity has degenerated into a constant quest for newness and change for their own sake. It is often blindly believed that whatever is new is better; the latest car is better than the older model; the new system is an improvement over the old; the new style is preferred to the old style. Likewise it is believed that whenever there is a change, there is progress; and the quicker the change, the better. Consequently, we look for new ideas to make new systems and new forms and eventually to reach the so-called New Heaven and New Earth.

But there is a pitfall in this quest. It is to identify change with progress, and newness with goodness. Not all the changes we make can be honored as progress; only the change that enables us to move closer to the goal can be called progress. So, we must have goals. Without a goal, we cannot determine whether the change is progress or the new is an improvement. Our goals constitute the criteria for self-evaluation and provide the signposts to guide us toward our destination. Goals represent something that we value so dearly and uphold so strongly that they become part of ourselves. Thus, our search for maturity is in fact our pursuit of goals and values. Man is by nature a goal seeker. Whenever his goals become obsolete, he searches for new ones.

Twentieth-century man has been characterized by a cartoonist as a tall, well-dressed, well-fed, well-developed young man looking out over a wide landscape at a huge question mark which hangs over the distant horizon as if it were a magnificent star guiding his way. He is not sure where he will go; his future is incalculable; he does not know what he really wants. His soul no longer rests upon secure foundations. He has lost his sense of security and balance. He is driven to smoking, to excessive drinking, to tranquilizers and drugs which relieve him from unbearable feelings toward life. Increasingly, he feels that he is at the end of his tether. Western society has taken on a new dynamism around which the whole world is rushing. It sweeps like a hurricane over every corner of the earth and every aspect of human life. Our world is in constant turmoil, full of voices without cohesion or focus. Man is bewildered. He is unsettled, lost, without goal and destination.

But life is a pilgrimage. We are always on the road, and there must be a goal at the end of our journey. There must be a holy place, a shrine, or a temple at which life's pilgrimage culminates. On the road we perpetually ask, Where are we going? But we experience the futility of setting goals in this ever-changing world. We find goals meaningless, for, even if we set them, they cannot remain long without being swirled into the common tide of change. So we are floated away by the tide purposelessly, passively, and apathetically. This is one of the most serious symptoms of spiritual sickness today. Without goals, life is meaningless. Goals give hope to man. Without hope, life is unbearable. So we must search for goals. We must search for values. We must search for hope.

The weakness of the present-day ethos is its orientation to the here and now. It values the present at the expense of the past and the future. Without the root of the past and the perspective of the future, one is confused, bewildered, and lost forever. In the midst of an ever-changing tide, a college student can only say, "Confusion is a choice word to describe my position." What we need in education today is "utopia thinking." [3] "Utopia" is often regarded as unattainable, beyond human capability, or even fantastic. But this should not be the case. Utopia thinking emphasizes the importance of goal-seeking, purpose, and the future.

A group of high school students were asked to write an essay on their ideals for the 1970's, but the students were more concerned about whether *there will be the 1970's* than they were with what is going to be *in* the 1970's.[4] Under the threat of total annihilation by nuclear weapons and universal pollution they deemed the future of mankind hopeless. Their faith in the future had been undermined. Without faith in the future, there can hardly be goals. A lack of goals blocks the discharge of one's energy, for no goals means no channels for creativity. Therefore, no matter how uncertain our future, we must have goals.

One's goals come from his ideals, and one's ideals from his values. Values are formed out of the life experiences that one treasures. Others may or may not evaluate them in the same way. If one's experience is indelible and brings ineradicable satisfaction to him, the value is formed once for all. Otherwise, it needs to be repeated until it is assimilated as a value. No wonder, then, that—in an age in which change is constant—it is hardly possible to repeat the same experience again and again as though something permanent and constant is inherent in it. In reaction against the traditional, authoritarian, static social order, the modern trend is toward the other extreme, which exalts change and progress over goals

and stasis. Dynamism becomes blind dynamism because
it does not have goals. "Change Is King," but this king
does not have sharp insight into the future. Thus, value
revolution goes on and on.

In an address to the Philosophy of Education Society, it
was said that clearly stated normative principles to deal
with antinomies of education are the most urgent need in
the contemporary philosophy of education.[5] One may
question the feasibility of having clearly stated normative
principles of education in this highly pluralistic society.
However, unless "pluralism" is considered synonymous
with "normlessness," there would be no question about
having norms. If pluralism is not anarchism, there must
be norms, even if these norms are subject to modification
and change. Social norms are based on common goals
that are deeply rooted in our common values and aspirations. The lack of clear principles of education is in a
sense due to the bewilderment about value in the present
age. Confusion about values in education has existed for
over two decades. It manifests the bewilderment about
values on the part of society as a whole.[6]

Recently, Rollo May has indicated that the prevalent
anxiety on campuses and elsewhere in society is caused
by the disintegration of values in our present-day culture.[7] The feeling of inability to cope with this disintegration arises because there is no longer a unifying core
within us. The values and goals that in past centuries
provided a unifying center are now found to be irrelevant,
and there are no new ones to take their place. We are in a
state of transition from the old to the new. We live in an
era in which the old king has been dethroned but the new
king has not been found. We are on the threshold of a
new era of values and goals. Today the task of education
is to provide a climate in which the nourishment and
growth of values can occur, and our task is to rediscover
the core of values that bind us together. To accomplish
this task, the study of the concept of maturity is urgently

proposed, for it epitomizes human aspirations, goals, and values.

Businessmen are often regarded as financially-minded and concerned mainly with the development of their business. But in an article "Science, Cybernation and Human Values," [8] it is pointed out that businessmen today are equally baffled by the question, Where are we going? and by the lack of purposeful direction. Businessmen are not exempt from the quest of what ought to be, because they are also human beings. The quest for ideals, goals, and direction is part of human nature. Social scientists take values into consideration and are equally concerned with the questions, What ought to be? and, Where are we going? In seeking to understand the causes and effects of human behavior, social scientists recognize that there is no value-free sociology. Sociologists must have concern for what the healthy community is going to be. It is proposed that social scientists seek to establish the universal sociopsychological norms of community balance, health, and sanity far removed from the traditional balance.[9] How can these universal sociopsychological norms be established? The search for a universal goal is indispensable. Without a common goal, there will be no common norms. Without common norms, the communication between the West and the rest of the world cannot be fruitful; conflicts between different cultures and ethnic groups cannot be resolved.

Scientists devote themselves to the discovery of reality, of what is, rather than what should be. They are more interested in objective facts than subjective ideals and goals. But when the scientist discovers what *is*, he cannot help asking what *should be*. It is no surprise to us that a book edited by the president of the National Academy of Sciences concludes with these words: "Homo sapiens, the creation of nature, has transcended her. From a product of circumstances, he has risen to responsibility. At last he is MAN. May he behave so." [10] This is a solemn expression of inner aspirations and ideals by the writer. "May he behave so" is not a statement of objective facts; it is a sincere prayer that implies unspoken ideals, norms, and goals for the whole of mankind. At the same time, it suggests that the childhood of mankind is over. We are in a new era in which man has transcended nature and can act responsibly as a man, a mature man.

As men, we must be concerned not only with the past and the present but also with the future of mankind. W. E. Hocking reminded us sometime ago that we live in the future; the effectiveness of our living depends on the sagacity of our forecast.[11] Present-day culture is too strongly oriented to the present, the here and now. Our present needs to be seen in relation to our future as well as our past. What is our future?

One may question the validity of comparing the individual life cycle with human history as a whole. Nevertheless, there is a parallel between the growing process of an individual person and the growing process of a group. From the historical study of Arnold Toynbee, it is concluded that the principle that is inherent in the creation of a new culture through the response of a creative minority to environmental challenge is similar to that of the manifestation of creativity in the individual person. If the challenge is too great, the creation of a new culture becomes abortive; if the challenge is just what can be accepted, a new culture is created by the group. This is also true of the growth of the individual person. This principle sheds light on our understanding of the future of mankind.

From the psychological point of view, the period of adolescence is the time of revolt in search of independence, identity, and self-determination. The adolescent demands the right to think for himself and to determine his own destiny instead of being under the constant supervision of his parents. He experiences rapid mood changes. He is unstable, impulsive, and unpredictable even to himself. He has a strong drive toward emancipation. He alienates himself from his parents. Parents sometimes find themselves treated with hostility and rudely challenged by a child whom they have loved unselfishly and still love. He rebels irrationally, for the sources of hostility lie among unconscious fantasies and conflicts from his early childhood. To the parents, adolescent rebellion seems a heartless desertion, a betrayal of confidence and love. Yet a youth goes through periods of disintegration and reintegration which culminate in adulthood. He grows in thinking and perception. He does not live in the unrealistic fantasy world of early childhood. Magical thinking is no longer good for him. He has now reached the stage of concrete and rational thinking.

The centuries since the Renaissance have been compared to the critical years of adolescence.[12] Since the sixteenth century, man has been awakened to his own right of self-determination. Politically and religiously, he did not remain content to be the slave of external authority. The Reformation affirmed the right of the individual to interpret the Scriptures for himself. Oppressed people began to seek independence: a series of revolutions took place—the French Revolution, the American Revolution, the Russian Revolution, and non-Western revolutions. The oppressed colonies achieved independence one by one. New nations emerged on the world scene and began to take active part in the world community and assert equality, freedom, and independence—India, Korea, Indonesia, and numerous other nations of the Third World. Revolutionary changes are taking place within the so-called underdeveloped countries, and struggle for independence and equality goes on in the United States in the form of the civil rights movement, the women's liberation movement, and the revolts of the American Indians. The process of democratization that took place within national states in the West in the nineteenth century has now extended to the world

scene. The non-Western peoples, comprising two thirds
of the population of the world, are emerging as active
participants in the world community. This struggle is the
adolescent search for maturity, and the process of democratization is a sign of its fulfillment. There is a growing
sense of independence, self-determination, freedom, and
equality.

The developed countries in the West have played the
role of parents in the drama of the struggles of adolescent
growth among non-Western developing countries. The
adolescent rebellion against parents is manifested in the
element of anti-Westernism in the revolution. Westerners are asked to leave the country. "Yankee, go home" is
the adolescent cry of "Leave me alone." But in this
process of maturation, the West has failed to play its role
successfully. The failure of the West in Asia and Africa is
the failure of inspiration. The West is spiritually bankrupt. While in Europe in 1919 Liang Ch'i-chao, who had
served as Minister of Justice and Minister of Finance in
several cabinets and was the central figure in the controversy over East-West encounter in China, was surprised
to find Westerners disillusioned with their own civilization. In a conversation with an American journalist,
Liang asked the man what he would do when he returned
to America. He answered: "When I go back, I shall shut
the door and wait. I want to wait until you have
introduced the civilization of China to save us." [13] The
Western rulers had no strong faith to offer those they
ruled. They dominated like immature, possessive parents
trying to exploit their children to satisfy their own
desires, and they insisted that their way was the only
way. Their spiritual bankruptcy was manifested in their
insecurity, domination, and aggression. Any financial
assistance was conditional. When non-Western nations
rebelled against them, they felt betrayed, instead of
accepting the adolescent rebellion as a natural phenomenon in the process of growth toward maturity. In fact,

Westerners too were searching for maturity. Now, they and their non-Western partners have grown together differently; one has learned to be less possessive, while the other has achieved independence, freedom, and to a certain extent equality.

Spiritually, the non-Westerners are bankrupt too. They too are disillusioned with their own traditional culture, which has not been able to stand the challenge of new Western dynamism. Both the Westerners and the non-Westerners are beggars, seeking for food to nourish spirit, soul, and mind. Today's generation has seen people working hard to get money, but failing to find happiness. "Spiritual goals in life are a lot harder to attain than a Cadillac" is the confession of one beautiful, wealthy, intelligent American girl.[14] Science and technology have enabled mankind to reach the concrete operational stage in which realistic thinking supersedes magical superstitious thinking. But this is not enough. Physically, it is excellent; spiritually, it is an inedible stone. In this time of crisis, mankind is in the making. But science and technology are merely tools. We have to search for goals and the spiritual foundation on which to build our goals. Somehow, we have reached our "adolescent" period together. The next stage may well be our mature "adulthood."

In order to understand our present era and to set future perspectives and goals, it is necessary to make a brief historical survey of the East-West encounter, particularly the Chinese encounter with the West. It is a long and fascinating story, reaching back into the pre-Christian era. No one knows for sure when the West first obtained knowledge of China. Perhaps it was sometime in the sixth or seventh century B.C. In 128 B.C., Chang Ch'ien was sent by the Chinese emperor Wu Ti into west central Asia for diplomatic relations, and eventually indirect trade between China and Europe developed. Silk was brought from China to the Roman world at the beginning

of the Christian era.[15] According to Pliny, Chinese iron
was also on the market in Rome. The Han dynasty used
iron weapons in driving the Huns to the west.[16]

Alice Chase has indicated that the soybean, known and
used in China since 2838 B.C., was introduced into France
in 1740, into England in 1790, and into America in the
nineteenth century.[17]

The significant direct East-West encounter took place
mainly in the East. Traditionally it is believed that the
apostle Thomas preached the gospel in China, but it is
the Nestorian mission that has substantial evidence. The
Nestorians reached China around A.D. 650 during the
T'ang dynasty and were honorably received by the Emperor. The Westerners were tolerated until A.D. 845,
when the missionaries were compelled to renounce their
missionary work, which allegedly perverted the institutions of the country.

Near the end of the thirteenth century, trade routes
from Europe to China were again opened because of the
Mongol conquest of the East. Kublai Khan, the ruler of
the eastern Mongol dominions, set up his capital at
Peking (Cambaluc) in 1264. There he received two Vene-
tian merchants, Nicolo and Maffeo Polo, who were com-
missioned by the Khan with letters to the pope asking for
one hundred missionaries to be sent to the capital. In
1275, the Polo brothers returned to Peking taking with
them Nicolo's son Marco. They served the Khan for
seventeen years, enjoying both honor and advancement.
At the end of the thirteenth century, they returned to
Europe and wrote *The Book of Marco Polo,* which gave to
the West its first comprehensive picture of China. Later,
Christian communities were established through Western
missionaries, but with the collapse of Mongol rule in
1368, they appear to have vanished.

During the sixteenth century, the Portuguese advanced
to Java, Siam, Indochina, and the southern coast of China
(A.D. 1514) seeking trade. An official Portuguese mission

was sent to China in 1517, but the Chinese attacked and destroyed the Portuguese trading port at Canton in 1522 because the Westerners were reported to favor conquest rather than peaceful commerce. Driven from Ning-po and Amoy, the Portuguese traders established themselves at Macao, and the Chinese constructed a wall with one gate in order to control the movement of the Westerners. The Chinese merchants at Canton desired to trade with these lawless Portuguese. Consequently, trade prospered, but diplomatic recognition was ignored.

In 1582, Matteo Ricci, an Italian mathematician and astrologer, came to Macao as a Jesuit. He was at first garbed in the robes of a Buddhist monk, but later, in the garments of a Confucian scholar. He was allowed to reside in Peking and he preached with considerable success. He prepared for the Chinese a map of the world with China in the middle. The Jesuits made use of every intellectual, scientific, and mechanical device in appealing to Chinese officials. But some Jesuits were expelled from Peking because during the Ming dynasty Neo-Confucianism was inclined to be fixed and intolerant. The Manchu rulers were not in favor of this exclusive, dogmatic, authoritarian Roman Catholicism.

During the seventeenth and eighteenth centuries, the Dutch dispatched four embassies seeking diplomatic relations with the Manchu rulers, and commercial concessions from them, but the ambassadors were asked to perform the most humiliating nine prostrations (*kowtow*). Following the Portuguese and the Dutch, the English arrived in China in 1637, the Danes in 1731, the Swedes in 1732, the Russians in 1753, the Americans in 1784.

Early in the seventeenth century, English authors began to show their knowledge of China. Sir Walter Raleigh included two judicious comments on China in his *The History of the World* (1614). Robert Burton leaned heavily on China for examples in his work *The Anatomy of Melancholy* (1621). The first English drama that used

China for its theme was the tragedy by Elkanah Settle describing the conquest of China by the Tartars. The play was performed at the Duke's Theatre in 1674. After a visit to China in 1637, Peter Mundy summed up his impression by saying that no kingdom in the world was comparable to it in these particularities: antiquity, size, wealth, health, plenty, arts, and government. During the eighteenth century, adoration for China was less marked. Samuel Johnson approved of, but refused to exalt, the civilization of China. The height of regard for China could be seen in the words of Sir William Temple, who was attracted by Confucius and considered China as a model empire, perfect in its institutions, the symbol of an orderly society.

In 1711, some of the works of Mencius were made available in French. The Sorbonne became the headquarters of the Chinese cult. Many Jesuit scholars admired Confucius as the master, the most learned in moral and political philosophy, who accepted the same God as the Christians. Montesquieu frequently mentioned Chinese civilization in his writing. Voltaire was an outstanding French exponent of Chinese culture. *I-Ching* was translated by François Duesnay, who saw the value of education in the natural law, with China as the model.

In Germany, an awareness of China was intensified by the philosopher-mathematician Leibniz, who learned about China from the Jesuits. He wrote to Claudius Philip Grimaldi asking about useful Chinese plants to be transplanted in Europe, Chinese medical knowledge unknown to the West, and the possibilities of translating Chinese historical books into Latin for the improvement of the West. Philosophically, he accepted certain Chinese principles and reasoned that the Chinese *Li* (substance, being, entity, principles, or laws) was the equivalent term for the Western God. Goethe composed *The Chinaman in Rome* in 1796, showing his impatience with those who held romantic attitudes toward China. But as he grew older, he became aware of the importance of China, a "valuable country," "a place where he [Goethe] can flee in case of need." Of his poems entitled *A Hundred Beautiful Women*, three were related to the Chinese and their problems.

From 1500 to 1800 the relations between the East and the West were, on the whole, conducted on terms established by the East. During the sixteenth century, the Western nations were never in a position to impose their will on the imperial rulers of China. The Westerners of the industrial age, impressed by their own scientific and technical achievements, no longer felt inferior to the Chinese. Western thinkers of the nineteenth century increasingly looked upon the countries in the East as backward, undeveloped, and retarded, in need of Western conquest. During the last three decades of the nineteenth century, the differences between the East and the West increased. Never before had the West been so far ahead of the rest of the world in scientific and technological skill and in living standards. It is understandable that Westerners began to feel superior. The philosophies of the nineteenth century led to a relativism that put all values, religious or moral, into question.

Western influence in the East has not come to an end. It will find expression in forms different from those of the past. Because of the Western impact, the structure of life in the East has been greatly changed and is continuously changing. In some respects the change is revolutionary. The rise and intensification of nationalism in the East is the most powerful force awakened by Western aggression. The East has been saved from falling entirely under Western domination by training itself to resist, using a Western weapon, industrialization. The West itself is undergoing a profound and striking transition. Consequently, the East is in the process of two revolutions— i.e., that brought on by Western impact and that shared with the West in the process of growth. In what way these forces will shape the East and the West no man knows. It depends upon how both the East and the West respond to them. However, it is clear that the nineteenth and twentieth centuries have ushered the East into a new era.

Soon after World War II, Edwin A. Burtt visited the East on behalf of the American Philosophical Society. He had been active in East-West dialogue and made a generous remark about Chinese tolerance, openness, receptiveness, and assimilation of foreign cultures. He observed that Western science and philosophy were the two prime objects of absorption by the Chinese and predicted that China would absorb as rapidly as she could everything in the West that seemed fruitful to her and would reinterpret her heritage accordingly.[18] As we observe what has happened on the mainland of China and in other parts of Asia, in the past few decades, we can hardly tell what will be the result of East-West encounter. But it is clear that a new soul is awakening in the East as well as in the West. As an American historian and missionary to China for many years, Kenneth S. Latourette concluded that Communism was by no means the final stage in China's revolution; there would be other stages, although no one could know what these would be. However, he was certain that when China moved into them, that for which America had labored would not be entirely lost, but would be assimilated in a living, growing China in altered form.[19] What will be the final stage in China's revolution? The answer to this question needs to be worked out in the context of East-West encounter. China can no longer remain a hermit kingdom. She is an indispensable part of the world community.

Kipling's poem has been quoted often in books, lectures, and banquet speeches whenever the issue of East-West encounter is involved. Sometimes it is quoted fully, accurately, and in its proper context. Now and then it is extracted partially, used mistakenly, and misunderstood. Kipling's words are challenging and forceful.

> Oh, East is East, and West is West, and never the
>     twain shall meet,
> Till Earth and Sky stand presently at God's great
>     Judgment Seat;
> But there is neither East nor West, Border, nor
>     Breed, nor Birth,
> When two strong men stand face to face, though they
>     come from the ends of the earth! [20]

Perhaps because he is overwhelmed by the enormous social problems of immigrants from India, Pakistan, the West Indies, and other parts of the British Commonwealth, Géryke Young, in *Two Worlds—Not One: Race and Civilization,* emphasizes the difference between East and West in support of segregation—"never the twain shall meet." East and West are diametrically opposed to each other in their approaches to world order and concepts of knowledge. In spite of his segregationist view, he cannot help acknowledging that East and West share one basic aim: both Easterners and Westerners search for a single unitary principle by which the unity of mind is restored and the multiplicity of the world becomes a meaningful whole.[21] Therefore, basically he too acknowledges that it is one world we live in, not two. The twain shall meet.

Every generalization about the characteristics of East and West has some truth in it, but none is entirely true. Often it is said that East is mystical, whereas West is rational; East is religious, whereas West is scientific; East is intuitive, whereas West is intellectual; East is spiritual, whereas West is materialistic; East is centripetal, whereas West is centrifugal; East is static, whereas West is dynamic; East is courteous, whereas West is frank; East is passive, whereas West is aggressive; East is past and future, whereas West is here and now; East is renunciation, whereas West is fulfillment; East is self-suppression, whereas West is self-expression; and so on.[22] But, as we observe carefully, Easterners and Westerners each possess the characteristics of the other to some extent, though each group is shaped to manifest its own strong characteristics. East is East, and West is West, but the twain come from the same origin, having in common basic human nature. Easterners would enjoy a high standard of living as much as Westerners do. As a living person, the Easterner *can* become dynamic, because the static Easterner also has the dynamic force inherent in him.

Despite international conflicts and the mounting threat of nuclear warfare, the world is becoming *one*. In this jet age, distance ceases to divide East and West. But physical closeness is no guarantee of authentic encounter and dialogue for the peace of the world and the realization of world community. Wherever we go, the problem of man is the center of human inquiry, and one of the basic issues in the problem of man is the concept of maturity. It is also a question of Where am I going? which implies man's unique yearning for future direction. As Hendrik Kraemer observed from his firsthand experiences of the East as a missionary, and of his own West, "Orient and Occident are both in the process of re-evaluation of themselves and of one another." [23] In this process of reevaluation, the study of the concept of maturity is essential in knowing one another's basic aspirations. Because of the cross-cultural invasions between the East and the West, a new form of world civilization is emerging; whether it will be singular, as W. E. Hocking predicted,[24] is uncertain. But one thing is clear: the study of the concept of maturity in East and West is significant in the search for common goals and values. The following pages are devoted to a brief survey of the concept of maturity in psychology, Christian theology, and Chinese philosophy for those modern "migrant birds" who are seriously searching for an image of the mature person, of becoming mature, in the context of East-West encounter.

# II
## Psychological Maturity

WE LIVE in an age of science and technology, and psychology is the science of mental processes and behavior. Therefore, in our search for maturity, it is essential for us to study the concept of maturity from the psychological point of view before we can understand it in Christian theology and in Chinese thought.

There are two approaches to the concept of maturity. One is to look at it from the static perspective; the other, from the dynamic point of view. The first examines it as a state of *being;* the other sees it as a process of *becoming.* In fact, the two approaches complement each other.

Semantically, "maturity" comes from the Latin word *maturus,* which means "ripe." It derives its meaning metaphorically from horticulture; it signifies the state of full growth, full development, and perfection. But in this age of realism, maturity as a state of full growth, full development, and perfection is often an unwelcome idea. The tendency is to equate maturity with maturation. It is argued that when emotional maturity is understood as an ideal state, it is something like truth, beauty, and goodness to which one can aspire but which one can seldom achieve.[1] In the strict sense of the word, maturity means the degree or the quality of maturation at a certain stage in the process of human growth.

Older persons are not necessarily mature. For some, growth has been arrested at certain points in one way or another. They do not have the special qualities of a mature adult in their dealings with themselves, with other persons, and with issues of life. The process of human growth is ever changing. We find that the chronologically mature person is not always psychologically mature. Occasionally, we find younger persons who are quite mature intellectually, emotionally, and spiritually. Since age does not fully express maturity, our search for it is a continuing process.

Carl R. Rogers is an exponent of the process-oriented approach to emotional maturity. He disagrees with those social scientists who see the good life as a fixed state of reduced tension and the achievement of equilibrium in the midst of life's competing claims. From his practice of client-centered therapy, he concludes that the good life is a process, not a state of being; a direction, not a destination. The good life is not a state of virtue. It is not a condition in which the individual person is adjusted, fulfilled, or actualized. Rather, it is the process in which the human organism determines to move in a particular direction, out of internal free choice.[2] This process-oriented approach reflects Western dynamism. Emotional maturity is an ever-changing process because we can never reach absolute perfection in this world. Even a professed Chinese Confucianist in his late eighties acknowledges that he has not achieved the state of maturity he sets for himself. He tries to keep his mind open to new ideas and changes in life by getting in touch with young people constantly.

In daily conversation, someone remarks, "Mr. So-and-So is a mature man." This brief comment does not specify an ideal state in the absolute sense, but rather a state of excellence which commands our attention to its relative perfection. Consequently, it is also proper to regard emotional maturity as a state of maturation which is relatively perfect for that stage. To regard maturity in this way does not necessarily imply ideal perfection, which is unrealistic and unreachable. In refuting the idea that maturity is a state of being, we need to be aware of the danger of thinking of maturity as nothing but process, that is, a process without direction and goal.

Heraclitus, the ancient Greek philosopher, is known for his process-oriented emphasis that everything is in the process of change, like the flux of a stream running toward the sea. Even though we stand constantly at one spot, the stream of time is ceaselessly changing. But this metaphor has its limitations when transcribed into daily life. If everything were constantly changing in the literal sense, we would not be able to recognize our schools, offices, homes, cities, friends, and even dear ones. Within the process of change, there is always a certain degree of stability, permanence, and immutability. Things are indeed constantly changing, but this must not be taken too literally. It is possible to see things from the perspective of an ideal state which signifies direction and goal for the process. However, this ideal state is not fixed; it is realistic and subject to modification in the process of maturation.

In spite of the fact that maturity as an ideal state of perfection is seldom appreciated or reached, it is still worth striving for. When we discover that it is unattainable, we can revise the goal according to our capability. Lest we should be discouraged, we need an image for our future becoming. This image represents our ideals, goals, and values. Without a concept of maturity, we do not know where we are going or how well we are doing. If we want to live our lives meaningfully, we cannot live without it.

Physicians too are increasingly aware of the lack of ideals, goals, and values in modern living. They are not satisfied with the overemphasis on prolonging life through scientific research and medical expertise. We are warned by a medical authority not to "continue to ignore the prophets of old and the Greatest Teacher, who knew that life is judged by its meaning and not merely by its duration."[3] So far, research has been mainly on the biological study of man for the prolongation of life rather than for fuller and happier living. Prolonged life is not necessarily happy and meaningful. Without meaning in life, old age is hard to bear. Cancer research is important, but research on the quality of life is equally important. This testifies to the significance that the concept of maturity bears on our understanding of the meaning and quality of life. Health should not be seen primarily from the physical point of view. The World Health Organization defines it as "a state of complete physical, mental, and social well-being."[4]

Words such as "health," "normality," and "well-being" are all related to "maturity." They are almost synonymous in some respects. Our major concern is not to define them accurately but to find basic criteria for knowing whether a person is psychologically healthy, normal, and mature. Psychological maturity is defined differently by various psychologists: Sigmund Freud, Carl Jung, Alfred Adler, Karen Horney, Erik Erikson, Erich Fromm, Gordon Allport, Abraham Maslow, to mention just a few. Marie Jahoda, in her study of the current concepts of mental health, classifies all factors that characterize mental health into six major categories.[5] They also represent basic qualities of psychological maturity because the distinction between mental health and psychological maturity is just a matter of degree. These qualities can be summarized into two mutually related, interacting categories: (1) internal integration and harmony and (2) external integration and harmony. The distinction between these two categories is made for the purpose of discussion and understanding, but in reality they are inseparable.

## 1. INTRAPSYCHIC INTEGRATION
### AND HARMONY

The first umbrella title that covers the intrapsychic characteristics of a mature person and their manifestations is "internal integration and harmony." The healthy mature person brings all parts within himself together into a complete and harmonious whole that is organically in order. It matters not whether they be called emotion, volition, conscience; feeling, reasoning, judging; mind, soul, spirit; or consciousness, subconsciousness, unconsciousness; or even the id, the ego, and the superego. Functionally, they may be affection, volition, perception, and cognition. In a healthy mature person, there are no barriers or conflicts among them. They are in coherent harmony with one another, though they may be misunderstood as separate entities without mutual correlation. To reach internal integration and harmony is a never-ending process. The person who is mature is internally integrated and integrating, harmonized and harmonizing.

What are the manifestations of one's internal integration and harmony, and how are they expressed? To list them one by one would be to compose another list of Beatitudes. Affectively, it is manifested in one's self-acceptance, self-confidence, self-esteem, and self-respect. Volitionally, it is manifested in one's autonomy, independence, self-determination, freedom, sincerity, spontaneity. Cognitively, it is manifested in one's unified philosophy of life (identity, integrity). Perceptually, it is manifested in one's accurate perception of oneself, purposiveness, self-objectification, and a sense of humor. Each category does not stand by itself. All are interrelated and integrated. In fact, the distinction among them is unrealistic. The characteristics listed are those which can be attributed to the internal integration and harmony of mature persons.

The process of human growth is often divided into

childhood, adolescence, and adulthood. This distinction again is to be taken as artificial because the growing process is dynamic, and at some points a person may regress to early childhood. There is no clear-cut day or month that psychologically divides childhood from adolescence. Man's growing process is continuous, though it may at times shrink back or become arrested. For an understanding of psychological maturity, the study of the process of human growth itself is important, but it is beyond the scope of this book.

At the moment of birth, a baby becomes a separate physical entity with psychic raw materials for the construction of a new personality. He or she is like a piece of clay in the hands of a potter. Through the senses the infant interacts with the external environment, including personal beings (mother, father, nurse, siblings, relatives, neighbors) and nonpersonal objects (bed, toys, chair, table). Every interaction with the external environment has its particular impact on the creation of mental images. Images are formed in the mind like small islands emerging on the ocean, and become parts of the child's consciousness. These separate islands come together as a continent, "a continuous land-mass of consciousness," [6] as Carl Jung calls it. This process of coming together is a kind of internal integration and harmony. In the process of human growth, the psychic elements seek to get together in forming a coherent whole. Every new interaction with the environment adds new elements to the psychic self, but they must be integrated into the whole. On the other hand, every new interaction brings about further differentiations, and in turn further differentiations require greater integration and harmony.

Of all interactions with the environment, the interpersonal relationships are the most significant psychologically. By the way in which a child is fed, caressed, or fondled, he forms images of others as well as of himself. The consistency of the relationship reinforces the consolidation of the images being formed. This process of the consolidation of the mental images of oneself and others can be considered also a kind of internal integration and harmony. As one grows, his mental images become more complex, and in the process of integrating mental images, one finds meaning, and all come to make sense. When mental images do not develop because of lack of external stimulation, or when mental images are too fragmented to be integrated successfully, the person is in trouble. When this internal integration is successful, there emerges one's selfhood as an individual. Thus, one's internal integration and harmony is manifested in his individuality, which is "the alpha and omega of Jung's system." [7] Individuation is the central task of childhood. To become an individual is essential in any democratic society.

When one integrates his own self-images, the question Who am I? will be answered, and ego-identity is found. The process of integrating one's own images is particularly critical during adolescence in modern society because of increasing mobility, disintegration of institutions, and multiplication of subcultures. Successful internal integration leads to the formulation of one's integrity, which Erik H. Erikson considers to be the mark of maturity.[8] The failure of internal integration and harmony leads to adolescent identity diffusion and despair in adulthood. Conflicting self-images can occur because of inconsistencies in the way one has been treated by other people who love him one day and hate him the next without any particular reason. What is important is not their words, mannerisms, or actions, but the quality of emotion they convey. Inner conflicts lead to lack of integrity, self-hatred, and despair.

As one grows into maturity, he develops his "style of life" which is so important in Alfred Adler's emphasis on individual psychology. Each person has a unique style of life, just as each person has his own particular self-image. Each person's integrated self-image is unique, because no two persons can have similar life experiences of the same emotional quality, even if they are twins. Ego-identity refers to a conscious sense of individual uniqueness, the unconscious striving for continuity of experience, and solidarity with one's group. It also implies the continuity of meaning that one communicates to others around him and those key figures in his life. It is, however, not something so fixed that nothing can be changed once it is formed. Since the internal integration and harmony is an ongoing process, ego-identity is subject to modification when there are significant new interactions with the environment. There will be a combination of the old and the new, and then a new sense of identity will emerge.

This integration of self-images is affectively manifested in self-confidence, self-respect, and self-esteem, which is by no means identical with arrogance or pride. Lack of these qualities can often be traced to anxiety. A sense of pride, arrogance, and self-assertiveness can often be traced to the same root. They are disguises of inner anxiety and insecurity. According to Karen Horney, the analysis of neurotic personality in relation to anxiety has great importance.[9]

Furthermore, we can trace the root of anxiety to unhappy interpersonal relationships in early childhood in the family in which there is no warm, authentic, self-giving love. Anxiety is caused by the lack of true love, which creates self-alienation and inner conflicts. Paul Tillich added a religious dimension to the analysis of anxiety, but lack of love is still its concrete cause. No love means no security, and no security is anxiety. To overcome insecurity, one tries to idealize himself, thus creating inner conflicts between the true self and the idealized false self. When one is loved, this effort of self-defense becomes unnecessary. Only love can give man inner security; only love can integrate the divisive self and bring unity to each individual. Thus the internally integrated person shows self-confidence, self-respect, and self-esteem.

Self-confidence is manifested in calmness, equilibrium, and steadiness. The internally integrated person is calm enough to face unexpected accidental shock, and strong enough to resist external pressures. He can meet the external challenges and threats that might cause him to despair. The psychologically mature person does not panic easily under unusual circumstances.

Critical of Sigmund Freud's sex-oriented interpretation of human personality, Alfred Adler points out that the will to power is the main drive in human behavior. Thus, man is always plagued by a sense of either inferiority or superiority. The sense of inferiority is dominant in childhood because a child is helpless and has to be dependent on his parents, who are superior and powerful. However, no matter whether we interpret personality growth in terms of sex instinct or willpower, man is consciously and unconsciously in search of internal integration and harmony. Man's inner conflicts manifest themselves in his inferiority complex, his superiority complex, or his Oedipus complex, and block his psychic energy for creativity. It is not enough to bring unconscious inner conflicts to the conscious level, but one must work out some kind of integration and harmony. The inferiority complex is caused by the lack of love. When one is loved, he feels important. He no longer feels inferior; he has no need to become superior to anyone. Thus, love makes internal integration and harmony possible. When one is internally integrated, he is a person in his own right.

Volitionally, internal integration and harmony is manifested in autonomy, independence, self-determination, sense of freedom, and responsibility. As one grows from childhood to adolescence, his psychic energies are united and become a strong stream of force for constructive tasks. He then becomes an inner-directed person. The center of his personality is rooted within. He feels more active; he is less inhibited; he becomes increasingly free and spontaneous; he is flexible to move and to adjust. But this is not a kind of superficial flippancy or self-surrender in his social contacts. His life is marked by his "functional autonomy," independence, self-determination, and responsibility. He has self-chosen values and goals, an inner core in his personality; he is not a spineless creature; he does not react impulsively; he draws all factors together and responds to them responsibly. He is no longer childishly other-directed. On the contrary, he is self-directed. He is his true self.

In the process of moral development, a child absorbs moral values from his or her parents by identifying with the parents through the interpersonal relationships. This can also happen with other authority figures in the extended family in the same way. In the beginning, the morality of children is heteronomous. They behave properly because their parents require it. The center of their morality is not rooted within them, but in those authority figures who represent the moral values of the society. By the process of identification, parental moral values become internalized, and the childish heteronomous morality is transformed into autonomous morality during the adolescent period.

To use Sigmund Freud's terms, the *superego* functions within each person as a moral agent of the society. It exercises its power in discriminating what is right and what is wrong, like a hidden judge enthroned within us. It is commonly understood as conscience. It is our second consciousness. The first consciousness is our *ego*, which synthesizes, organizes, combines, and unifies our mental processes. The other psychic force is the *id*, which is like a chaotic caldron full of the seething energy of the instincts. The ego stands for reason, whereas the id symbolizes the untamed passions. The relationship between the ego and the id can be compared to that of the rider and his horse. The id supplies the necessary energies, while the ego has the privilege of deciding on the goal. The superego sets the rules and regulations for the ego to follow. The id strives for satisfaction according to the pleasure principle, while the ego must observe the external world and lay down an accurate picture of it by reality testing according to the reality principle. From the Freudian point of view also, the healthy mature person is one who has achieved internal integration and harmony. In this case, he is the one who integrates the three psychic forces within him, namely, the id, the ego, and the superego. The ego is not overruled by the id, nor is it overly punished by the superego; it is in good harmony with both. Appropriately, Freud's dictum, "Where *id* was, there shall *ego* be," is paraphrased to read, "Where *superego* was, there shall *ego* be." [10]

The symptoms of mental illness are the manifestations of internal disintegration and disharmony. The ego of the healthy mature person functions properly in its reality testing and in its organizing and coordinating psychic forces within him. It is freedom from excessive anxiety, alienation, inhibition, and conflicts. It has power and strength for autonomous action as well as strength to resist tension and frustration. Internally integrated and harmonious, the mature person is spontaneous, honest, and sincere. Likewise, he is in no need of proving anything to himself and others. He has the freedom to be relaxed and to be less serious about himself. He has won the "peace with honor" within him. Increasingly, he is less uptight, so that he is able to give himself a chance, the freedom to take risks, and the spontaneity to be unpretentious. He can laugh at himself, because he is reconciled with his true self. He is able to say: "Behold, I am happy. I feel good. I am O.K." His inner security is so great that he does not feel threatened by the criticism or questioning of others. He is not hypersensitive or defensive. This happens because he is internally integrated and harmonious. Since he has inner unity, he can afford to criticize himself and take corrective measures accordingly. He can bear "the experience of sudden change with certain equanimity and serenity." A well-known world leader and scholar had lived through mental pain and physical suffering. At times, it looked like the end of the road. "But," he said, "I have gone through it, and I have more stability and equilibrium now." He accepted his limitations and the finitude of life. He was happy that he was not omnipotent.

In the early stage of human development, juxtapositions of ideas exist in the primary thinking process. Later they are integrated in the secondary thinking process. Particularly during adolescence, this cognitive integration makes one rational. Any conflicting ideas need to be sought out. The central problem during middle life is to integrate one's spontaneous philosophy of life with one's acquired philosophy of life in order to achieve a mature view.[11] The spontaneous philosophy comes from our life experiences, whereas the acquired philosophy is the total accumulated from others through formal education or informal contacts. One characteristic of a mature person is his unified philosophy of life. He has worked out an integrated system of values for decision-making, determination of goals, and moral judgments. President Lowell of Harvard University was asked how he was able to make so many important decisions in a single day. He answered: "Oh, it is not too difficult. There are only a few—perhaps half a dozen—principal standards of value by which I make my judgments. Almost every decision fits into one of these broad categories." [12] A successful lawyer (in his sober reflection after fifty years of practice) said without reservation that the most immature persons he had met in the practice of law were those incapable of making decisions themselves. Their weakness is their lack of a unified system of values. They allow the juxtaposition of various values and ideas to exist in their minds. They are confused, indecisive, and unsettled.

Teleologically, the lack of a unified philosophy of life is manifested in one's lack of goals and direction. The mature person is goal-oriented. He knows what kind of person he wants to become; he is capable of postponing immediate satisfaction for long-range goals. In his *Becoming,* Gordon W. Allport expounds how the man who strives to become the person he wants to be and to reach the goals he chooses for himself is internally integrated around a core, or "proprium." He has a sense of future direction.

Great men have definitely ordered and selected goals.[13] They do not hit blindly. They travel toward a port of destination selected in advance, or toward several ports related in succession. This is echoed by the study of F. Barron about the "soundness" of graduate students at the University of California at Berkeley. Among the traits that stand high on the checklists are "integrated pursuit of goals" and "persistence." [14] Rollo May also finds that the distinctive quality of the mature healthy person is his integration around self-chosen goals.[15] He knows where he is going.

Because the mature healthy person has definitely ordered and selected goals, he is capable of concentration and becomes a highly productive person. He makes best use of his potentialities, powers, energies, and opportunities. He is best in becoming a "self-actualized" person, from Abraham H. Maslow's point of view.[16] The mature man lives by his inner laws and does not surrender to external pressures. He is autonomous and does not allow himself to be controlled by the approval or disapproval of others. What matters most is his own approval. He is his own boss. He uses all his talents and capabilities to the fullest. He is the most ethical of all people in the sense that he regulates his own actions according to his inner principles rather than following popular notions. His morality is autonomous. His ethics may not be the same as the ethics of the people around him, but he certainly has his own ethics. He is such an autonomous person that he sometimes acts like an alien in a foreign land or like a spy engaging in espionage. He hates to become hypocritical for the sake of superficial social adjustment.

Being internally integrated and harmonious, the mature healthy person is likely to develop his potentialities to the fullest. But he does not do so in order to sell his creativity in the market of manpower. He is not a commodity to be exploited like a prostitute. He is not market-oriented in Erich Fromm's sense. He is not alienated from himself. He is a man who can say, "I am what I do."[17] He sees himself as an actor. He is one with his powers. His creativity can be released smoothly along integrated channels that signify the goals and ideals of the actor. He may not be as "successful" as his unscrupulous neighbor, but he has security, autonomy, integrity, and spontaneity, which makes him less vulnerable to changing fortunes and external pressures. He does not violate his moral and intellectual integrity, lest he should weaken and even paralyze his total personality. He does not betray his inner self. But his autonomy must not be misunderstood as egoism. His autonomy is the key to his productivity and creativity. He breaks the frontiers in his chosen fields. He is a unique gem of the society, the pioneer of the unknown, and the vitality of stagnation. He has a sense of worth. But he is not too proud of himself.

In the process of human growth into maturity, internal integration and harmony is not a separate factor. It is tied in with external integration and harmony.

### 2. REALITY PERCEPTION AND SOCIAL MATURITY

One who is internally integrated and harmonious is also externally integrated and harmonious. The categorization of the two is merely for the sake of discussion. In fact, it is nonexistent in actual human behavior because the internal and the external are integrated and harmonious with each other. They are more than two sides of the same coin which is inorganic and impersonal. Man is an organism, a personal living being. In this personal living organism, the internal and the external are integrated and unified. His internal creativities and productivities are manifested externally in his interactions with the environment. He does not shut his energies within himself. His internal energies find external expressions in his multiple involvements and participation. Although he is autonomous, independent, and self-determinative, he is not an isolationist. He has self-love, but his self-love is manifested in his love for others. He is self-confident and self-respectful, but these qualities are manifested in confidence and respect for others. His realistic perception of himself is matched with his realistic perception of other people and of external reality. He finds his own identity. Likewise, he finds his community. He is internally integrated and externally harmonious, and his external harmony is expressed in his reality perception of the external reality and interpersonal relationships.

The psychologically mature person can be detached from himself and see things objectively. He is capable of self-objectification. Objectivity is essential for reality perception. His perceptual relationship with external reality is not distorted, because he is able to see himself objectively. When he sees things objectively, he sees them as they are rather than as he wants them to be. He is capable of perceiving the truth and of comprehending the true meaning of the speaker rather than what he wants to hear. Perceptually, a mature person is realistic even though he has his own ideals. He is integrated and harmonious with reality not only internally but also externally. Reality perception requires healthy physical conditions as well as a healthy mental state. Reality can be distorted by psychic needs, but the internally integrated and harmonious person is likely to be free from such distortions. Consequently, he is accurate in his perception of the physical environment. The perception of a mature person tends to be ego-transcending, self-forgetful, and unselfish. Objects are perceived as having independent reality of their own. It is not necessary for him to dominate or to conquer the external world in enhancing his sense of superiority in compensation of his sense of inferiority. He respects facts and sees them as an integrated and unified whole rather than as scattered fragments. Since his perception is comprehensive, he is less susceptible to seeing the partial truth as the whole truth. His respect for the integrity of external reality makes him less likely to show favoritism unjustly. All things hang together as they are, and he sees them as they really are. A psychologically mature person perceives well.

Now and then a person's integration and harmony is manifested in his sense of humor. He is relaxed not only with himself but also with others. Although he is surrounded with difficulties, he does not feel overwhelmed. On the contrary, he can see the situation objectively and laugh at it without cynicism. His sense of humor is positive and subtle. When he shows it, nobody is hurt. Neither does he humiliate himself to please others. His humor is neither masochistic nor sadistic. Rather, it is healthy. This sense of humor is related to one's self-objectification.[18] It is a joyful discovery of wisdom in an unusual way. The mature person possesses it in one form or another. His sense of humor is part of himself. He does not sell it as a comedian or consciously try to make himself humorous. His humor comes out spontaneously and naturally. His sense of humor is always an outgrowth of his wit and inner harmony.

In his interpersonal relationships, the mature person is honest, trustful, patient, tolerant, considerate, responsible, and loving. In these ways his external integration and harmony takes concrete forms. He is honest not only with himself but also with others. His honesty stimulates and invites others to show their honesty to him in return. He is willing to talk things over with his children, his marriage partner, and those who come in contact with him. He is in harmony with external reality and not threatened by it. He trusts his children with responsible tasks, but his trust is not blind trust. His trust is in proportion to the trustfulness of others. In the same way, his trustfulness stimulates and invites other people to be trustworthy. His external integration and harmony brings about other people's internal integration and harmony. He does not become angry easily or quickly. He respects other people's ideas, opinions, and rights to be uniquely theirs. It is difficult for him to impose his own ideas on others, not because he is incapable of doing so, but because he is against it.

The mature person, in tune with other people's feelings, is truly considerate. He is more than superficially polite or courteous. A head nurse is so mature that she says to a weary and overworked assistant: "You have worked all day and all night. I want you to go home and have a nice sleep." She is considerate of her colleagues and knows how they feel. She is a boss, but not bossy. She does not demand the last bit of energy until her subordinates are fully exploited. She feels responsible for them as well as for the patients. Their well-being is her concern. She cares for them because she loves them. Love implies care, responsibility, respect, and knowledge. Genuine love makes her relate to others in a way in which is found the paradoxical nature of man, that is, the desire for concurrent closeness and separateness of each person. Love implies mutuality.

When someone asked Sigmund Freud what a normal person can do well, Freud did not give a sophisticated or highly theoretical answer. He simply said, *"Lieben und arbeiten"* ("to love and to work").[19] A mature person should be able to love deeply and work productively. This simple formula expresses a mature person's external integration and harmony. Love is not an abstract thing. Erik Erikson points out that when Freud said "love" he

meant genital love. Genital love demands a love object of
the opposite sex for its fulfillment. Human morality
develops from heteronomy to autonomy, but human
sexuality grows from autoeroticism to heteroeroticism.
In early childhood, one is narcissistic. A child is
self-centered, like Narcissus, who pined away for love of
his own reflection in a spring. The small child is full of
fantasies and considers himself as omnipotent as his
father. But in the course of personality development, he
becomes awakened to the necessity of "altruistic surrender," recognizing his dependency upon the love and
power of the parents. He is no longer so egocentric, nor
so omnipotent. The process of human growth is a kind of
liberation from self-centeredness. As one grows into
maturity, he becomes aware of his object-interest and less
narcissistic.[20]

In maturity, we enjoy genital love, but it can be most
painful if we are deprived of our love objects. This is
what makes the broken love affair so tragic. We have all
been warned not to seek happiness solely from genital
sexuality. But this does not stop the mature person from
seeking his love object in others, especially those of the
opposite sex. He cannot be so self-centered that he
remains isolated from other fellow human beings. In the
process of human growth, we become increasingly other-
directed and outreaching. We seek our love objects in the
external world in finding a more satisfying relationship
with more people of more races and nationalities until we
identify with the whole of mankind. The more mature we
become, the less narcissistic we are.

No psychologist would advocate self-centered rugged
individualism. Alfred Adler's individual psychology is not
individualistic. He points out that human sexuality is a
symbolic expression of the individual's relation to the
whole of mankind.[21] He emphasizes the proper cultivation of social interests and social adjustment. Whether a
person functions well or not is measured in relation to the

welfare of the whole of mankind. Anything worthwhile should be worthwhile for all. So his individual psychology can be regarded as social psychology as well.

Carl Jung's "individuation" is not self-centered. Certainly concern for other people is implicit in his psychology. Also, Abraham Maslow's "self-actualization" is not self-centered. On the contrary, the "self-actualized" person possesses "all-embracing love for everybody and for everything."[22] In his *The Mature Mind,* Harry A. Overstreet proposes the "linkage theory of maturity," which emphasizes human relatedness. In contrast to rugged individualism, he points out that we must grow from egocentricity to sociocentricity, because we are not mature until we have both the ability to see ourselves as one among others and the willingness to do to others as we would have them do to us.[23] Our emotional maturity is equivalent to our capacity to love others in an adult way, which is not self-centered. Our emotional maturity depends on the degree of affirmativeness in relating to other human beings. To hate is emotionally immature. The quest of supremacy either individually or collectively is a sign of immaturity because it is self-centered and endangers one's external integration and harmony. The society that is characterized by the search for supremacy through mutual destruction is immature because it overemphasizes egocentricity and distorts individuality.

The mature person is open to all possibilities in his environment. His life is characterized by multiple participation in his community, professional organizations, and voluntary associations. He expands his interests endlessly: sports, art, music, furniture, architecture, antiques, literature, and so on. A top business executive became interested in learning how to repair television sets and found it intriguing. He had actively participated in community activities in one place where he lived, and hopes to do so in a new community after his retirement. The external integration and harmony of this mature executive is manifested in his readiness to meet new situations, new problems, new ideas, and new people in the world. He quickly learns new skills and new patterns of behavior in effectively solving his problems.

The mature man is so at home in this world and with himself that he is not afraid of new cultures, new customs, and new ways of life. Because he is externally integrated and harmonious, he likes travel and enjoys the beauty of nature. He appreciates the variety of cultures and welcomes the challenges of new frontiers. Although he is venturesome, he is not an imperialistic aggressor. His attitude is neither hostile nor exploitative.

In psychological literature, "the extension of the self" and "environmental mastery" are used to describe the characteristics of the healthy mature personality,[24] but they have the connotation of a one-way conquest of the external environment. The attitude behind "extension" and "mastery" is likely to be misunderstood as that of supremacy and domination, which reflects childish egocentricity. But, in fact, the healthy mature person is the less egocentric. "The extension of the self" implies the loss of the self in the cause of sacrificial nature, whereas "environmental mastery" indicates the capability of adapting and adjusting to situational needs. They signify external integration and harmony.

In brief, psychological maturity is an ongoing process which includes an ideal state of intrapsychic integration and harmony, which is manifested in reality perception, social and vocational adequacy, and aesthetic sensitivity.

# III
# Christian Maturity

IN OUR UNDERSTANDING of the West, the study of Christian maturity is indispensable. The Judeo-Christian heritage is one of the major streams that constitute Western civilization. It reflects the kind of understanding of the nature of God which shapes one's view of human history and one's patterns of life. In this post-Christian era of the West, Christian influence is by no means negligible, though it may take a secularized form in our daily lives. In fact, psychological maturity is not much different from Christian maturity in form except that the latter is based on a theistic conviction. This is clearly manifested in the interviews with mature Christians. They may use Biblical expressions or symbols to describe their maturity, but in essence it can be identified as psychological maturity, if it is expressed in nonreligious terms.[1]

Experientially, Christian maturity is an ongoing process whose ultimate fulfillment is beyond human history, and yet it operates in time. It is tied with the Kingdom of God internally and eschatologically. Christian living is centered on the Kingdom of God concept, which is a theonomous state, a theocentric rule, which is "in you" now and yet to be realized in the future. Christian maturity represents a Christian ideal, a perfection, an ultimate goal that can never be achieved in this world. Partially, it is realized in history, but it transcends time and space.

Christian maturity is not a sum total of virtues that
constitute laws and regulations for living. Rather, it is a
forward-going process marching toward the consummation of a new creation made possible by divine intervention in history, in the incarnation in Jesus Christ.

In psychological terms, immaturity is often implied by
all forms of mental illness; neurotics and psychotics are
immature persons. In theological terms, immaturity is
likewise indirectly implied by negative words such as
"sin," "unbelief," "flesh," "selfishness," "jealousy," "im-
purity," "dissension," "enmity," and "licentiousness."
Maturity is expressed in positive words such as "faith,"
"hope," "love," "joy," "peace," "gentleness," and "new
creature." Now, let us turn to the quest of the functional
characteristics of Christian maturity to see whether the
proposition that the mature person is internally and
externally integrated and integrating, harmonious and
harmonizing, is also valid from the Christian point of
view.

### 1. Faith, Integration and Harmony

"A Christian" is "a believer in Jesus as the Christ."
Consequently, in our quest of the characteristics of
Christian maturity it is right to begin with "faith." A
believer is one who has faith. Faith implies two major
aspects of living, the cognitive and the affective. Cognitively, faith is synonymous with doctrines, creeds, and
other forms of propositional content about the ultimate.
From the affective point of view, faith is identical with
trust and commitment, which signifies the internal integration and unification of our psychic energies into a
single channel. It is the resolution of inner conflicts, the
purity of heart, the peace of mind, which brings joy and
hope. Faith is the key that releases invisible power within
a person who is divided and at odds with himself. It

relieves the wretchedness of the man who experiences conflicting powers within him that are tearing him apart. Faith liberates a person from this agony of inner conflict and gives new birth to his personality. A man of faith is a new creature. (Rom. 7:7–25; John 3:1–15; II Cor. 5:17.) Christians affirm that faith is a divine gift. The presence of the Spirit within human spirits makes this internal integration and harmony possible. The Spirit, who transcends time and space, operates in human personalities, which are bound by all creaturely limitations and finiteness. Christian maturity is, in this sense, a divine gift. It is more than psychological maturity. The Christian internal integration and harmony is unique, though functionally it may be similar to psychotherapeutic processes. Its uniqueness resides in the focus of this integrating, unifying, and harmonizing process of psychic forces. The focus is Jesus Christ, who is the center of Christian faith. The most ancient credo in the Christian community is "Jesus Christ is Lord." To nonbelievers, Christians are intoxicated with Jesus Christ. From the point of view of nonbelievers, Christians are crazy, because the nonbelievers cannot understand the peculiar patterns of behavior caused by belief in Jesus Christ.

A person's Christian maturity is not measured by his contribution to the institutional church, faithfulness in religious observances, or position held in ecclesiastical structures, though these can be true expressions of Christian maturity. The measurement rather is based on the degree to which our whole being finds integration and harmony around the sole center of the Christian faith, Jesus Christ. He is the mature Christian and the mature man. He reveals to man the true human nature. He is truly human. The mature Christian integrates and unifies his philosophy of life with one focus, Jesus Christ. His religious faith is not to be exploited either by himself or by others. He goes to church not for the sake of getting social prestige, making new friends, or expanding business contacts, though these are legitimate outcomes of his religious life; he goes to church primarily because he integrates his whole living around his faith. (His religion is "intrinsic" and not "extrinsic.")[2] He does not use his faith to improve his status or his income. His faith is not a means to an end, because there is no such alienation between means and ends. His faith is lockstitched into the whole fabric of his being. For him, there is no conflict between his faith and his daily living, because the two are integrated. This does not mean that he does not encounter inner conflicts, but when he does he resolves them around the center of his faith. However, nobody is completely integrated. Everyone has elements of disintegration in all dimensions of his being.[3] Perfect integration nd harmony is only an eschatological possibility, which 'eyond the space and time of this world.

sus Christ is often looked upon as the greatest t ner of rules and regulations to be followed in reaching th te of maturity. He is sometimes presented as a per model to be imitated carefully in our growth (as the t of the Christian classic by Thomas à Kempis, *Imitat f Christ*, indicates). But the stage of imitation is our tual childhood which is characterized by heterono here is the conflict between what is to be obeyed an one can obey. So long as this conflict exists, there lf-estrangement and alienation. When Christ is a m to be imitated, one has to strive consciously for t ealization of this goal. This is an inevitable stage, bu s not a mature stage in which one can say, "Christ live me and I in him." At this level Christ and "I" are in ated, unified, and harmonized without losing individu and integrity of personality. This unity and integratio dynamic, flexible, and subject to modification whenev he living Christ and "I" so determine. This integration d harmony is not the selfless state that is often p d by mystics in their ecstatic experiences. (Christ is n erely a great teacher or a model who exists externally; rather, he is an indwelling personality whom Christians call the Spirit. The living Christ is an internalized being for mature Christians.

This happens unconsciously, spontaneously, and freely. A Christian in this stage is no longer proud of his works, virtue, and merits, because these are the characteristics of the previous stage of justification by works. He is now in the stage of justification by grace through faith. Christ is not known through dead propositions or doctrines, or even moral codes to be discussed and obeyed. He is the living presence, the source of spiritual power and energy, which quickens and transforms human personality. By being integrated with this source of power, human effort seems trivial and insignificant. Therefore mature Christians feel relaxed, spontaneous, and free. After all, it is salvation by grace and not by works. The goodness of the mature Christian comes out naturally. He behaves unpretentiously. He is ready to be asked any questions. He makes no effort to hide himself. The interviewer would feel it unnecessary to tell such a person that whatever is said would be confidential. This spontaneity reveals true autonomy, which is not something one has to fight for consciously and constantly. One lives as a free child of God and not as an enslaved servant.

Mature Christians know who they are. They are aware of the identity that signifies their peculiar existence in the world based on their religious faith. Being a Christian may not be prestigious in a non-Christian society, but a Christian would strongly affirm the identity that implies his special role in the drama of human history. Christians are here to take part in the mission of their Lord in the world, to do the impossible task, and to hope for the consummation of all by divine grace. Their identity cannot be destroyed either by fire or by the sword. They are not ashamed of being Christian even though they are threatened with persecution by the rulers of this world.

Their strong sense of identity is accompanied by their undefeatable integrity which stands the temptation of political power, material wealth, and worldly pleasure as well as the conquest of military aggression.

The word "integrity" scarcely occurs in the New Testament, but it is one of the most essential themes in the teachings of Christianity.[4] It is one of the characteristics of Christian maturity. It is a manifestation of the internal integration and harmony of mature Christians. They are "afflicted in every way, but not crushed; perplexed, but not driven to despair; persecuted, but not forsaken; struck down, but not destroyed."[5] For the sake of Christian identity and integrity, a Chinese Christian was willing to endure the pain of parting with his beloved fiancée because of recent political upheavals. In his reflection a few years later, he showed no regret; not because he later found another girl, but because it was right for him to do so. He knew who he was, what he should do, and where he was going. Although it was painful, he was able to make a decision and accept its consequences. Because of internal integration and harmony, one has the "courage to be,"[6] the courage to affirm his existence, and the basic human right to be a person.

What makes the Christian faith Christian is its Christocentricity, and not theocentricity in general. Not all theisms are Christian. Even the "God" who appears in Mark Twain's imaginative and sometimes wildly funny book *Letters from the Earth* is not particularly Christian, though the idea of God is based on the narrative of the Old Testament, which is the cradle of the Christian faith. The jealous tribal god who demands nondiscriminatory slaughter of his people's enemy is a scandal to modern men's conscience, and is far removed from the God revealed in Jesus Christ. Christian identity and integrity is rooted in Christocentricity rather than in the narrow, exclusive, and sometimes clannish deity who destroys the innocent for the preservation of his people.

The classical term that signifies the Christian striving toward total salvation is "sanctification." It is still strongly upheld by pious, conservative believers but has lost its attraction for liberals. Karl Barth described it as "the claiming of all human life and being and activity by the will of God for the active fulfilment of that will." [7] The will of God is the center of Christian living. This God is not a tribal god; he is the God revealed in Jesus Christ, that is, God the "Father." No one knows the Father except the Son (Jesus Christ, who suffered under Pontius Pilate, was crucified, buried, and rose again from the dead). No one knows the Son except through the Holy Spirit, who comes forth from the Father and the Son, because the Father and the Son are one. And so Christ asks for his followers that they may be one "even as thou, Father, art in me, and I in thee, that they also may be in us" (John 17:21). The will of God is that they may become perfectly one—"I in them and thou in me, . . . so that the world may know that thou . . . hast loved them even as thou hast loved me" (John 17:23). Christian monotheism is unique because it is trinitarian monotheism. Christian perfection is the perfection of oneness among the Father, the Son, and the Holy Spirit: One-in-Three and Three-in-One. The secret of this oneness is love, for God is love. The Christian identity and integrity is derived from this dynamic, personal oneness which cannot be understood mathematically. Mathematical oneness does not integrate and harmonize multiplicities, because it does not have the dynamism of personality. The Christian God is the living source of personality because love is his nature.

The closest Greek equivalent to "mature" is *teleios,* which comes from *telos* ("end," "goal"). *Teleios* means "having attained the end or purpose, complete, perfect." There are passages where maturity is set in contrast to childhood, and where "full-grown" or "mature" is a justifiable translation of *teleios*.[8] (Eph. 4:13; I Cor. 14:20.)

In this contrast, children are not integrated in their thinking. They are "tossed to and fro and carried about with every wind of doctrine, by the cunning of men, by their craftiness in deceitful wiles." The full-grown, mature adult is Christ, who is the head. Jesus is the mature man (*teleios anthrōpos*). Likewise, God is termed *teleios* (Matt. 5:48). Christians are expected to be perfect as their heavenly Father is perfect. In other words, they must be mature as their heavenly Father is mature. The quality of perfection is the perfection of love.[9] This perfection of love is manifested in the integration and harmony among the Father, the Son, and the Holy Spirit—one God in three persons. The key to the understanding and realization of this seemingly unattainable perfection of internal integration and harmony is faith. Man's attainment of the perfect integration and harmony of the divine Personality is both an ongoing process and an eschatological possibility. Its realization is dependent on divine grace rather than on human effort. It is faith that makes the divine-human encounter possible. By faith, man becomes one with God. This faith is also expressed cognitively in the unification of one's theological system, which makes one less vulnerable to be tossed around by different teachings.

## 2. LOVE AND COMMUNITY

Internally, Christian maturity is faith; externally, Christian maturity is love. The Apostles' Creed begins, "I believe in God the Father Almighty." But the almightiness of God would be incomprehensible if it were understood as military power that would destroy the enemies of his people. It would also be contradictory to the perfection of God revealed in Jesus Christ who is the Father of love. If the almightiness of God had been preserved in the creed as the projection of man's will to power, it would be a sign of immaturity. In the process of religious development, it can be said psychologically that the religion of power reflects the childish fantasy of omnipotence, that the religion of holiness (separation) reflects the adolescent search for identity, and that the religion of love reflects the adulthood intimacy. If "God the Father Almighty" had been another form of childish assertion, "My father is greater than your father," it would be a relic from the past which the apostles had not expunged. God's power is the power of love, and his perfection is the perfection of love. Love puts things together, but the will to power strives for domination. So often, God is misinterpreted as a miracle worker who exercises his power to satisfy the desires of those who pay him homage. This is the worst kind of narcissism.

For some people, Christianity is outmoded and irrelevant to the modern age. In heteronomous childhood, authoritarianism is well accepted, but it is the target of attack during the adolescent period. As a child grows into maturity, heteronomy is replaced by autonomy. Modern man is in search of autonomy in opposition to any form of oppression, including oppressive religions. Christianity is no exception, because it has been presented by authoritarian evangelists in oppressive ways. They want to crush the wills of their hearers until they "repent." Conversion is described by religious psychologists as the resolution of conflicts which comes by way of the surrender of the penitent.[10] Emil Brunner sees that sanctification lies in following the steps of Jesus Christ in his self-surrender on the cross.[11] The use of the term "surrender" is often misleading. It implies that God is the conquering king who demands the absolute submission of his enemies and subjects. The almightiness of God is understood as power. But in fact his almightiness is his love. God is the loving father who wants to establish personal relationships with his people. If the relationship is based on love, it does not come about through conquest. The defeated may surrender outwardly but still hate the conqueror and strive for revenge. If the basic nature of God is love, this analogy of "surrender" does not do justice to the very nature of the Christian faith, to say nothing of its irrelevancy as a means of communication in the present age of democratization.

Certainly, the loving Father does not want the disintegration of personality of his growing children by keeping them completely docile and incapable of making responsible decisions. He gives his children maximum freedom in making choices so that they may become responsible persons. Slavish obedience kills the emerging personality of youth. If the church continues to preach subservience, the growing youth will surely rebel. To stay in that childish institution is against the inner cry for autonomy —a cry so strong that it cannot be stopped. Pharaoh cannot keep the growing people of God as slaves forever. The exploiter cannot resist the power of love to liberate the slaves, who are entitled to grow into maturity as responsible persons. It would be a tragedy if God were projected as the tyrant who ruthlessly usurps the birthright of his people to become mature persons. It is even worse if God is conceived of as a dictator of modern times.

The perfection of love is manifested in Jesus Christ in an unusual way. It is the way of self-defeat, humiliation, and lowliness, the way of suffering and death. The basic principle is that "he who loves his life loses it, and he who hates his life in this world will keep it for eternal life" (John 12:25). This paradoxical perfection of love is exemplified in the life of Jesus. The word "love" is used in many ways, such as "making love," "love your neighbor as yourself," "I love you," and so on. In the discussion on love, agape (self-giving love) is often set in contrast to eros (sensual love), as though agape is good and eros is evil. It is often asserted that Christian love is agape and not eros. But in fact, agape and eros are inseparable. There is no self-giving love if there is no self.

On the other hand, there is no selfhood if there is no self-giving love. The fulfillment of selfhood is in giving the self for others. Self-love is self-giving.

This paradoxical nature of self-giving love is also manifested in nature. "Unless a grain of wheat falls into the earth and dies, it remains alone; but if it dies, it bears much fruit." (John 12:24.) The selfishness of man is the source of his loneliness. But when he has the courage to sacrifice, he finds the salvation of life. The grain of wheat sets out the paradoxical truth of life. He who loves his life and stores it up as a personal treasure loses it thereby. Only he who hates his life—not in the sense of self-hatred, but in the sense of being willing to lay it down for others—will keep it eternally. Selfishness is stultification (cf. Mark 8:35; Matt. 10:39; 16:25; Luke 9:24; 17:33). The cross is the concrete symbol of self-giving love and the pattern of Christian maturity. Self-giving love breaks through with liberating power, but it does not demand acceptance by violating another person's integrity. This self-giving love has no strings attached. It is freely offered and must be willingly received.

History is full of stories of the self-giving love of mature Christians, although there are egoistic corruptions of love in the Christian churches also. The authentic sacrifices of missionaries in other lands should not be discredited or devalued because of Western colonialism and exploitations of Asians, Africans, and Latin Americans. In a mission hospital, only sacrificial love can make effective the healing of the sick. A picture of a missionary's wife giving some of her skin for transplant on a seriously burned boy of another race and nationality inspires medical students and other natives of that land. The act of going a second mile always brings joy to suffering patients and neighbors. A needy patient discovers money in his bed left there anonymously by a compassionate physician. Flowers from a nurse's garden cheer the incoming patient. An uncared-for old man is brought meals by a neighbor. A poor widow and her five children receive material support year after year from unrelated neighbors. Somewhere in the world, sacrificial love is always being given and received. But the perfection of sacrificial love is hard to attain in history, because it is something that "can have meaning only if the dimension of life is known to transcend historical existence." [12] Love so easily degenerates into an egoistic utilitarianism or into selfless mystical flight from historical contingency in search of union with the divine. In history, nonviolence cannot stand violence, as the cross of Jesus indicates. Agape love is something that transcends history and can only be fulfilled by transcending history. Sacrificial love does not fit into the social ethics of balance and competition, because it is grace and not law. Grace fulfills the law and transcends it. Sacrificial love often falls victim to human egoism which makes self-assertion an ethical norm, but in essence it belongs to eternity. Therefore, the validity of sacrificial love can be measured only by faith. It is not a wisdom of this age and it is folly to the rulers of this world. Nevertheless, it exists in the world and challenges the world. Agape is the final integration and harmony of life with life, which needs to be understood eschatologically. It is the perfect integration and harmony with the divine will.

Just as human body, mind, and spirit are integrated in constituting a living organism, agape and eros are united. Any suggested dichotomy between agape and eros is false. Self-love is legitimate, as pointed out by Paul Tillich and Erich Fromm. It is not as sinful as Reinhold Niebuhr indicated when he included it with the forces that "defy the inclusive harmony of all things under the will of God." [13] Self-love is synonymous with self-respect without which there is no wholesome personality. Self-hatred is morbid. Self-love comes from self-acceptance, and is the result of internal integration and harmony. It is expressed in legitimate anger when one's integrity is threatened, when one's basic human dignity is denied, and when one's personality is victimized. Self-love is created by agape love from others, which in turn becomes the basis of one's own agape love. Whether eros is interpreted as an egoistic sexual love in the entertainment world, or as mutual love in friendship (*philia*), or as the longing of all creatures for God as the highest good (in Augustine), it is inseparably intertwined with agape. A man in his forties whom I interviewed stated sincerely and reverently that Christian maturity is concretely expressed in his intimate sexual experiences. These blend his giving, his sense of responsibility for his partner, his care and concern as well as his openness to receive and to be loved. In actuality, eros and agape are integrated. They are not mutually contradictory. The conventional assertion that agape is good and eros evil is questionable. The sinfulness of man is his egocentricity which allows no room for the external world and other people. It causes man to make himself god. In the process of Christian growth, what needs to be eradicated is not eros. It is man's egocentricity which creates hell within him. Self-love should not be identified with egocentricity.

It seems that the separation of eros and agape comes from a one-sided emphasis on the transcendence of God and the total initiative of God in coming to man. Man's yearning for God is not recognized, and man's sexuality becomes twisted. According to ancient Greek mythology, Eros "seized his life-giving arrows and pierced the cold bosom of the Earth," thus creating life on the earth. Eros is the drive that pulls man toward the union of two individuals sexually, the urge that incites in man the yearning for union with the truth, the power that makes man reach out toward the object of love, the capacity that is expressed in our constant dialogue with the environment, the world of nature as well as the world of persons. Eros is not egocentric dominion over the love object. Eros is the passion of love which drives us out of our egocentricity. Agape without eros is a kind of grudging self-sacrifice, a legalistic obedience to the command of love which is far from living in faith and grace. There is no warmth and joy in this agape, because there is self-estrangement, inner conflict, and self-alienation. To separate agape and eros is to separate the inseparable. It is a reversion to the "either-or" mentality, the "me" and "non-me" differentiation in early childhood.

"Sanctification" has the connotation of holy, "to set apart as holy." But this setting apart does not mean isolation. It implies participation and involvement in the world. It is similar to individuation in human growth, to becoming a unique individual with special identity and mission. Sectarianism unfortunately is often saturated with "holiness," which is exclusiveness and isolation. It tends to pull the church away from the world. However, as pointed out by Paul Tillich, sanctification is character- ized by "increasing awareness," "increasing freedom," "increasing relatedness," and "increasing self-transcend- ence." [14] Sanctification does not make one secluded from his environment like a hermit; rather, it makes him more aware of the reality within and without. This awareness is sensitivity, insight, and realistic perception of ambigu- ous forces within and without. (In the process of sancti- fication, one becomes more in touch with his true self as well as the true selves of others. Consequently he is freer from the commandments of the law. He is less inhibited in the interpersonal relationships and moves toward mature relatedness.) He breaks through the walls of self-seclusion and reaches out to other persons. He accepts himself and is free from self-elevation, self- contempt, self-pity, or self-humiliation, because he is able to transcend himself under the impact of the Spirit. Self-elevation and self-contempt are two sides of ego-cen- teredness. Self-transcendence is a liberation from ego- centeredness. Thus, a decisive characteristic of Christian maturity is the power to sustain solitude and loneliness. Self-relatedness makes this possible. Self-relatedness comes from the integration of agape and eros and manifests itself in one's relatedness to others.

Love is the sign of Christian maturity. It is the state of increasing reconciliation with oneself and with others. It is the state of increasing resolution of the dichotomy between the self as a subject and the self as an object, and the state of spontaneous affirmation of one's essential being beyond subject and object. It is the state in which the search for identity reaches its goal and beyond its goal. Self-love and love for others are virtually one, the "courage to be oneself" and the "courage to be a part" are identical, and the polarity of the self and the polarity of the world are united and harmonized.[15] It is the state in which individuation and participation are integrated and become one process. In participation, one finds his individuation; and in individuation, one finds his true participation. This is not symbiotic in losing one's identity, integrity, and individuality, or in absorbing another's identity, integrity, and individuality. The polarity of the self and the polarity of the world come closer and closer until the two become one. Christian living is a process moving toward this state of being.

Christian maturity is manifested in Christian unity. "Relatedness with others" has a corporate meaning which is obvious. In his letter to the Ephesians, the apostle Paul points out that the unity of faith is no other than the attainment of Christian maturity. (Eph. 4:13.) But he does not consider the unity of faith from the individualistic point of view. For him, the unity of faith is always manifested in the context of the Christian community, the community of all believers, the body of Christ. Christian maturity is manifested not only in the ability to discern the true teachings from the false doctrines but also in "speaking the truth in love" and in the realization of one body, one spirit, and one hope. Christian maturity should not be understood as individual maturity; rather, it is the maturity of the body of Christ.

One Bible commentator points out that what is under

attack in Eph. 4:1–16 is eccentric individualism rather than sectarianism.[16] But this is doubtful, because sectarianism has hopelessly divided the church since the Reformation and will do so. Sectarianism is often based on the self-righteous, exclusive, partisan spirit, which brings disharmony to the church in all ages.

Individuality has its legitimate place in Christian maturity, but individualism does not. It is opposed to the corporate nature of Christian maturity which can only find its fulfillment in the Christian community. The teaching of the Bible is certainly against egoism and pride. In the life of Jesus of Nazareth, we find true humility, being born in the likeness of man, humbling himself as a servant, and dying on the cross. He is the embodiment of Christian maturity. By full participation in the life of Christian fellowship and the world, we grow into mature manhood and attain "the measure of the stature of the fulness of Christ." Holy Communion is the symbolic expression of participation in the body of Christ. Without this participation, there is no Christian maturity. Isolationism is a cul-de-sac no matter what form it may take. The religious mystics who isolate themselves from the rest of the world to indulge in ecstatic rituals are not mature from the Christian point of view, though they may claim to be so. The self-serving, secluded monastic life is not desirable if it aims at a complete withdrawal from this mundane world. Christian maturity is manifested not only in one's internal integration and harmony in obtaining identity and integrity, autonomy and individuality, but also in loving others and in participating in the fellowship of men in order to realize the relatedness of human nature.

We, as individuals and as nations, cannot achieve maturity and fullness independently, but only in interdependence and cooperation, in giving and receiving. We are always related, though we may pretend to be "little absolutes" and sometimes act as if we were small gods.

But this is contrary to Christian maturity. Sanctification is not attained in isolation, but rather in the community of believers, for we are related to one another. Paul Henry describes Augustine as a "great sinner and saint passionately in love with his fellow man, with Christ, and with God." [17] We are truly persons insofar as we acknowledge the full status of other persons as related to us. The natural movement of our personalities is not only centripetal but also centrifugal. Without communication with others, personality will wither, like a tree whose roots are cut off, or die, like a fish out of water. We are often subjected to the suspicion, ridicule, antagonism, and even persecution of others. No wonder we tend to withdraw from our potential enemies. But we must not, because it is by receiving the challenge of others that we are able to grow toward maturity. Sometimes communication with others may bring unhappiness, but without this communication there will be no maturity. Mature Christians are passionately in love with others and with God. They do not withdraw from God or from men.

No human being can come to maturity all by himself. To do so, one needs other persons. A distinguished professor of social ethics recalls that the turning point in his life came when the school registrar gave him a signature and commented that he would be a success, when he learned about others. Another mature Christian recalls that the turning point came to him when he learned the importance of other persons while he was weak and helpless in the hospital. Man matures only when he meets. Peter A. Bertocci points out that maturity of personality, maturity of religion, does not mean a "flight of the alone to the Alone" or "an emptying of self to Self." [18] It is the participation in "the eternal purpose of creation and growth of persons." It is to reach out and meet other persons trying to understand, empathize, and relate to them in a meaningful way. It is to realize that we are only partners to each other. A marriage partner may be the most important person in helping one to mature by mutual love, cooperation, mutual correction and challenge, and problem-solving. For the mature Christian, the new form of being is to become "the faithful covenant-partner of God," [19] in the accomplishment of his eternal purpose of creation. He needs to understand the divine partner and to see how important this divine partner is. This effort makes him less ego-centered in his whole being and doing.

To reach out and love hostile and malicious people, or to regard the world as our home and all the people in it as our brothers, is possible only if we learn to overcome the narcissistic tendency in us and to transcend our provincialism and narrow national loyalty. Humanly speaking, this seems impossible; but under the impact of the spiritual Presence, this can happen and has happened. This is the fruit born of the Spirit of love.

### 3. SECULARIZATION, INTEGRATION AND HARMONY

Is modern secularization a sign of maturity from the Christian point of view? To answer this question, we need to analyze the meaning and nature of secularization and the basis for judgment. The frame of reference is again the process of human growth. Early childhood is characterized by magical thinking. Selma H. Fraiberg appropriately names her book *The Magic Years,* which deals with the problems of childhood from birth to school age. As one grows from childhood into adolescence and then adulthood, gradually magical thinking is replaced by factual and rational thinking; myths are replaced by concrete facts; fantasies are challenged by realities; and heteronomy is transformed into autonomy. When one achieves individuality and independence, he is confronted with new crises: How shall he maintain his individuality and freedom? Which ties should he sever? Which should he keep, and which will be strengthened by his accepting responsibilities that his basic identifications would bring? As he grows through these crises, his view of life and the universe will be characterized by its unity, integrity, and the capacity for dealing with realities.[20]

Twentieth-century Christians search for the relevancy of their faiths to a secularized world. Can we feel at home in this secularized world? Should we accept or fight against secularization? Such questions emerge in our minds as we think about the world in which we live. We are often tempted to leave these questions to the experts and let them find answers for us, but this will not do. We are involved in the process of secularization, and there is no escape for us. We may like to ignore it, but we are bombarded with news of the secular city by the news media. We are pressed to think about it and its relation to Christian maturity.

What is secularization? It is the process of becoming secular. "Secular" means not religious, not connected with a church, not under monastic vows, temporal rather than eternal. "Secular" is the antonym of "sacred," which means holy, consecrated to a god or to God, hallowed. Secularization is desacralization. It is to make less religious, less church-connected, and more this-worldly. Religion is often considered to be something unscientific, irrational, superstitious, mystical, primitive, and otherworldly. If this is the case, secularization is not something evil. It can be a sign of human progress.

Cornelis A. van Peursen, a sociologist and lay theologian in the Netherlands, describes secularization as the emancipation of man "from religious and then from metaphysical control over his reason and his language." In his discussion of secularization, he points out three stages in the history of human thought. They are by no means clearly divided, and each contains some features of the others. They can be regarded as three types of approach to reality and ways of thinking. In the first stage (mystical stage), the subject is merged with the object and the two penetrate each other without much distinction between "me" and the rest of the world. It is the period of primitive society. In the second stage (ontological stage), the subject is differentiated from the object, and the sacred is separated from the profane. It is characterized by the "thinking of being as being." It is the period of the "divination of the gods" and the "humanization of man." It is also the period of feudalism. In the third stage (functional stage), the subject and the object come together. It is characterized by functional thinking which is pragmatic, concrete, this-worldly, nonmythical, and nonmetaphysical. God is considered to be too remote to have any impact on human lives. This is the stage in which most of us find ourselves. We are now liberated from supernatural beings, and what is real is that which is directly and concretely related to our life experiences. In each stage, there is danger; in the mystical stage, magic; in the ontological stage, substantialism; and in the functional stage, operationalism.[21] This observation does correspond to the process of human development, though we do not know what the next stage will be like. This shows that secularization liberates man from childish magical thinking and makes him feel at home in this world with less irrational fear. If this is true, secularization is to be welcomed.

Similarly, Harvey Cox describes the process of secularization in three stages, the tribal, the town, and the technopolis, which correspond to the mystical, the ontological, and the functional. Furthermore, he discusses how the Biblical faith has contributed to the disenchantment of nature by its Creation story, the desacralization of politics by the exodus, and the deconsecration of values by the Sinai Covenant.[22] Any form of idolatry, be it nature, nation, or emperor, is challenged by the Biblical faith. As a result, man is liberated from the bondage of fear and sees things from their proper perspectives.

Thus, man can "exorcise the magical demons" and perceive nature and the world as they truly are. Fantasies are gone, and man becomes a realist. In a sense, Christians are participants in the process of secularization. They do not absolutize anything and are concerned with this world without deifying it.

From the Christian point of view, the incarnation is the most decisive affirmative basis for secularization. The Word (*logos*) was made flesh in Jesus of Nazareth. He did not remain in the metaphysical sphere. On the contrary, he secularized himself and took on the form of man of whom Pilate said, "Here is the man!" (John 19:5.) His coming signified the beginning of a new era. He identified himself with the hungry, the thirsty, the stranger, the naked, the sick, and the prisoner. (Matt. 25:31–45.) He was not the god whom Camus, Nietzsche, and Marx understood him to be; he is not the god whose throne needs to be castigated by man in order to achieve human freedom, autonomy, and full responsibility; he is not the god who emasculates man's creativity and maturation. He is the secularized God who eats, sleeps, works, plays, and talks with men. Yet the people of Jesus' time did not know him. In Jesus, God identified himself with man without losing his divinity. His style was so secularized that the religious leaders at that time considered him blasphemous. His approach to the people was practical and concrete: feeding the hungry, healing the sick, and comforting the bereaved. For his mission, he organized a task group of men who were fitted for the job with an intensive training program. He manifested the utmost human maturity.

In him, we find the perfect integration and harmony of the sacred and the profane, the supernatural and the natural, true humanity and true divinity. "In him," says Karl Barth, "we encounter the history, the dialogue in which God and man meet together and are together." [23] In him, we find that the true God is the true partner of man and that the true man is the true partner of God. In him, the physical becomes spiritual, and the spiritual, physical; heaven and earth become one, and there is true reconciliation, restoration, and redemption. In him is true integration and harmony, for in him is love. In this perfect integration and harmony, the vertical and the horizontal become identical without falling into pantheism, that is, without losing identity. The dichotomy between the vertical and the horizontal ceases because the spacial analogy is inadequate for the transcendental, nonmetaphysical reality of love.

Mature Christians are realists in the true sense of the word. They have their two feet on earth and feel at home in the world. Despite all hardships and frustrations, injustices and cruelties, they actively participate in worldly affairs without becoming conformed to the world. They maintain the freedom and openness which secularization has brought to them. At the same time, they reject secularism as a closed world view which functions very much like the religion from which secularization wants to emancipate us. This freedom and openness come from the living God who allows no idolatry. They are at home in this spaceship earth, but they acknowledge that they are pilgrims participating in the course of history in which God acts. The kind of integration and harmony among God, man, and the world is similar to that of the Trinity—Three-in-One and One-in-Three. It is neither One-in-One nor Three-in-Three, for both come from the static concept of integration and harmony. The process of secularization has not been completed yet, because there are residues from the mystical tribal stage and the ontological town stage in the present stage of functional technopolis. The perfection of the integration and harmony of the Trinity is an eschatological possibility. The process of secularization will go on. As Cornelis A. van Peursen sees it, there will be a fourth stage, which cannot yet be known because we are still in this functional stage.

In the fourth stage, functional thinking may well be replaced by integrative and harmonious thinking. The fragmented pragmatic approaches are efficient in solving problems in some areas but utterly inadequate in others. Groups of specialists would find it necessary to get help from other specialists in different fields. Their openness and freedom would enable them to reach out to others for mutual assistance. The problems of pollution have awakened scientists and technologists to such need in solving problems. The solution of one problem is often the cause of another.

From the Christian point of view, God is the center of all integrations and harmonies, and he integrates and harmonizes in partnership with men who are his responsible and autonomous co-workers.

# IV

# Confucian Maturity

THE CHINESE have been taught to be proud of their civilization, which has been tested and developed for over five thousand years. It is held that the transition from tribal society to feudal society began when the Shang were conquered by the Chou during the twelfth century B.C. In order to consolidate the country, the Chou encouraged irrigation by the use of human ingenuity and talent instead of depending on magical prayers for rain. Consequently, man and his activities became more important than the spirits and deities. So they were kept at a distance. This led to the development of a humanism that stressed the unity of man and heaven. This humanism characterized the entire history of Chinese thought. It reached its climax in Confucius, whose ethics provided the spiritual basis for Chinese civilization.

Confucius, a descendant of a noble but poor family, was born in the state of Lu in the southern part of modern Shantung in 551 B.C. When the child was three, his father died. Confucius was a self-made man, and became the greatest teacher in Chinese history. His first name was Ch'iu and his last name K'ung. Traditionally, he was honored as the Great Master K'ung (K'ung Fu Tzu). He devoted his whole life to the teaching and training of character. In early adulthood he served as a minor official in the government of Lu. At the age of fifty he was made a magistrate and became the minister of justice, perhaps serving as an assistant minister of public works in the interim. As a result of political intrigue, he was forced to resign. For the next thirteen years he traveled from one state to another, always seeking opportunity to realize his ideal of political and social reform. Eventually he returned to his own state of Lu and in 497 B.C. died at the age of seventy-three.

Confucius had three thousand disciples. As a teacher, he transmitted to them the ancient cultural heritage. He was not a conservative transmitter of the past, but an originator of new ideas and new interpretations. He developed new concepts in which his superiors were not interested. He was at heart a social reformer. He was more than the ordinary literati of his time who made a living by teaching the Six Classics and acting as skilled counselors in the use of rituals at funerals, weddings, sacrifices, and other occasions. He set the pattern for the later development of Confucianism and made humanism decisive in Chinese philosophy. He was not interested in gods or spirits or life after death. His main concern was man and society, with good government and harmonious human relationships. He was more interested in the here and now, this world, than in the world to come. He was a creator as well as a transmitter, and became the founder of a new system of thought.

Maturity is an important underlying concept in Confucianism, which is essentially humanistic and anthropocentric. It plays a synthetic role in helping us grasp the wisdom of Confucius because it summarizes the image of an ideal Confucian gentleman, and is concretely manifested in the life of Confucius himself. It is expressed in different terms, such as *chün tzu* (superior man, son of the ruler) and *shen* (sage).

The discussion of this subject is based mainly on *The Analects* (often regarded as the most authentic work of Confucius), *The Great Learning, The Doctrine of the Mean,* and *The Book of Mencius.* As an approach to the subject, we may well center our discussion around two polarities: "self-cultivation" and "ordering and harmonizing the world." [1] They are similar to Paul Tillich's "courage to be oneself" and the "courage to be a part," which represent man's subjectivity and objectivity in the manifold dimensions of human existence. On the basis of these two polarities, we can see the integral relationships between the subjective aspect and the objective aspect of maturity in Confucianism.

## 1. SELF-CULTIVATION AND THE SUPERIOR MAN

Within the feudal social system, Confucius did not particularly emphasize the autonomy and independence of man as we know it in the West. He did, however, discover "the ethical individual," [2] and individuality certainly implies a considerable degree of autonomy and independence exercised by each person. The kind of independence that creates anarchy and indulgence cannot be found in the Confucian concept of maturity. Filial piety was highly exalted as an important virtue in the old days of authoritarian paternalism. It is in this context that the Confucian ethical individual is to be understood. The Confucian individuality does not imply the kind of independence and self-determination that is characteristic of rugged individualism in the West. From the Confucian point of view, man is always in relation to others and can never be thought of as isolated from the social context and community. This can be seen from Confucius' teaching of "self-cultivation" whose ultimate aim is the "ordering and harmonizing of the world." The cultivation of the ethical individual is not only for one's own sake but for the sake of others as well. It is not achieved in isolation, but always in close relation to one's social functions.

Functionally, the individual is an operating unit in the

family, the state, and the world. One's subjective maturity is the keystone in developing one's objective maturity with the world. Internal integration is the foundation for establishing external harmony. Therefore, in the process of maturation, one has to set his own household in order before he seeks to order and harmonize the state and the world. "The ancients who wished to show their fine characters to the world," said Confucius, "would first bring order to their states. Those who wished to bring order to their states would first regulate their households. Those who wished to regulate their households would first cultivate their personhood." [3]

What should one do for his self-cultivation? A systematic way of self-cultivation was suggested to those who wanted to follow it:

> Those who wished to cultivate their personhood would first achieve the rectification of their minds. Those who wished to achieve the rectification of their minds would first achieve the sincerity of their wills. Those who wished to achieve the sincerity of their wills would first extend their knowledge. The extension of knowledge depends on the investigation of things. When things are investigated, knowledge is extended; when knowledge is extended, the sincerity of the will is achieved; when the sincerity of the will is achieved, the mind is rectified; when the mind is rectified, the personhood is cultivated.[4]

The process of self-cultivation may be expounded in the different manner shown in the controversy in Neo-Confucianism between Chu Hsi and Wang Yang-ming. Whether the investigation of things comes before the sincerity of the will (Chu Hsi), or the sincerity of the will is prior to the investigation of things (Wang Yang-ming), a mature Confucianist is internally integrated and shows his sincerity to himself and to others. In the process of self-cultivation, the sincerity of the will and the investigation of things are mutually interactive and complementary, and neither one precedes the other.

The internal goal of self-cultivation is the "rectification of mind," which is a state wherein one is no longer buffeted by different views and ideas. When one achieves this state of mind, he is sure of what is right and what is wrong, what he should do and what he should not do. Although he is tempted to do wrong again and again, he does not show any sign of bewilderment or inner insecurity, because he is as sound and unmovable as Mount T'ai. He enjoys maximum inner composure and equilibrium.

From the affective point of view, the rectification of mind signifies inner confidence and a sense of security. From the cognitive point of view, the rectification of mind implies the unification and integration of ideas and thoughts and the consolidation of one's system of values. Affectively, the mature person does not fight and is able to mix with others easily because of his inner security. Cognitively, he does not agree with others completely, yet he is open to the opinion of others. Affectively, the mature man does not form cliques. But the immature man needs cliques for self-protection. Cognitively, the mature man is pleased by what is right. But the immature man can be pleased without necessarily being right. The immature man is what Confucius regarded as the *hsiao jen* (inferior man), and the mature man is *chün tzu* (superior man).[5] The rectification of mind is comparable to the unification of one's philosophy of life, one of the characteristics of psychological and Christian maturity. The individual's philosophy of life may be different from that of others, but its unification and integration are indispensable for any mature person.

To reach the goal of internal integration, one needs to extend his knowledge; to extend knowledge, one has to investigate things. From the Confucian point of view, to grow into maturity is to be engaged in the study of Chinese classics, in knowing the virtues of *yi* (righteousness), *jen* (human-heartedness), *li* (propriety), *chih* (wisdom), and *ming* (knowing one's destiny). Self-cultivation implies constant learning of all things, for there is always something to be learned. Every Chinese person is constantly advised to study hard and is reminded of the dictum, "There is no stopping point in learning." Self-cultivation does not mean only the cultivation of one's moral virtues, but means also the acquisition of knowledge, including all branches of human knowledge for living. It is true that "the superior man attends to the spiritual things, and not to the livelihood." But, on the other hand, Confucius said, "the highest degree of the spiritual is to know clearly the myriad things." [6]

The rectification of mind cannot be achieved merely through emotional education in interpersonal relationships or merely by training in methods and the process of learning. It requires knowledge of subject matter and content to be able to judge what is right and what is good. Without objective knowledge, one is often tempted by fantasies of all kinds. This is congenial to the psychological view of maturity in which a mature person is characterized by his accurate perception of reality and the Christian realistic assessment of oneself as finite. If one has factual knowledge, his perception is not distorted by his emotional needs; he becomes more objective in perceiving his own potentialities and limitations.

Confucius made an autobiographical statement to the effect that he began to study seriously at the age of fifteen and that he was able to stand (*lih*) on his own feet at the age of thirty. What does "stand" mean? Fung Yu-lan interprets it as the understanding of propriety (*li*) and the practice of proper conduct,[7] whereas Lin Yu-T'ang translates it semantically and psychologically as character formation.[8] It seems that the former sees the process externally, the latter internally. In both cases, to "stand" certainly implies the achievement of maturity which comes from self-cultivation through the investigation of things and the extension of knowledge. This brings to mind the parallel in Christian maturity expressed by

Martin Luther's famous affirmation at the Diet of Worms: "Here I stand." It is parallel to the courage to confess one's faith saying, "I believe in . . ." and "the courage to be oneself." But from the Christian point of view, this courage to stand and affirm one's faith is not by human effort but by God's grace, not a work but a gift. Because Confucian self-cultivation implies conscious effort, there is an element of stiffness, dryness, and legalism in it. But in the Christian "stand," there is an emphasis on the spontaneous, real driving force and the power of regeneration. Confucian self-cultivation assumes the basic goodness of human nature, whereas Christians stress the sinfulness of man which incapacitates human self-cultivation. One may suspect that Confucian self-cultivation is for the educated elite, whereas Christian faith is for all ranks of people. However, functionally both Confucian self-cultivation and Christian faith aim at the internal integration and harmony of psychic forces as well as ideas. This internal integration and harmony is an expression of *ch'eng* (internal sincerity and truthfulness). We can describe it as authentic human existence.

Self-cultivation is an ongoing process. Confucius did not stop learning at the age of thirty, but went on to describe his growth at the age of forty, fifty, sixty, and even seventy. Not only did he formulate his position, but went further in consolidating his position so that he had no doubts. He became an inner-directed person secure in his own conviction without being tempted by different doctrines and false teachings. He did not yield to social pressures, but was persistent in trying to realize his ideal goals of social reform. In his later years, he became disappointed and frustrated, but he never gave up. Consequently, he was known as one who knows that he cannot succeed, yet keeps on trying.[9]

At the age of forty, he had no doubts about where he stood. He would not sell himself for a high salary or for social prestige. He was a self-functioning person, individualized, and inner-directed.

At the age of fifty, Confucius was said to know the *t'ien ming* (the Decree of Heaven). This was a further step in his maturity. At the age of sixty he was obedient to this Decree, and at the age of seventy he could follow the desires of his mind without overstepping the boundaries of what is right.[10] His inner character was so transformed by the awareness of the Decree of Heaven that his life was totally identified with it. He knew his finite limitations and the purposeful force that works in and out of human life, the force that is beyond one's control.

As the tribal stage was transformed into the feudal, there emerged a monarchian conception of a supreme power differing from and superior to all other spirits and demigods. This supreme Deity was given two titles, T'ien (Heaven) and Shang-Ti (Supreme Ruler).[11] In the Classics, T'ien is used in five ways: (1) sky in contrast to the earth, (2) a ruling or presiding T'ien as referring to the Deity, (3) a fatalistic T'ien, almost synonymous with "fate," (4) a naturalistic T'ien, meaning Nature, or the power of Nature, (5) an ethical T'ien, the primordial moral principle of the universe. Often the second and fifth of these meanings are used by Confucius. T'ien is more impersonal than Shang-Ti. Chu Hsi (1130–1200), the Neo-Confucianist, remarked that the Decree of Heaven (T'ien Ming) in the naturalistic sense signifies the moral order of Heaven (T'ien Tao) or the Way of Heaven. Wing-tsit Chan, a modern Chinese philosopher, pointed out that the doctrine of the Decree of Heaven was developed by the founders of the Chou dynasty (1111–249 B.C.) to justify their rule. Their predecessors received the Decree but failed to do their duties. So the Decree of Heaven was passed on to them because of their virtue which determined human destiny.[12] The mature Confucianist knows the Decree of Heaven. "He who does not know *ming* (Decree of Heaven) cannot be a superior man." [13]

The superior man is most concerned about the Decree of Heaven; worldly success is not his primary interest. He takes what comes to him without complaint and accepts it as his portion in the total scheme of things. Because of this kind of acceptance, the "superior man" is always happy; the inferior man, sad.[14] This is very close to self-acceptance and self-understanding in modern psychotherapy. From the Christian point of view, one's limitations and mission in history are well signified by the doctrine of creation in which God is the creator and man the creature. The doctrine of calling implies that God is the Lord of history or the Lord of Heaven, T'ien Chu, which Roman Catholics use to translate "God" in Chinese. But the Confucian T'ien is not identical with the personal God of the Christian tradition. H. A. Giles, an English sinologist, compared the Decree of Heaven to the Will of God in Christianity. Confucius did not clearly define what the Decree of Heaven is, nor is the Will of God in Christianity clear in each historical context. Since the Confucian T'ien and the Christian God are not identical, the content of the Decree of Heaven and the Will of God cannot be the same. However, functionally both make one less egoistic and aware of the importance of acknowledging the objective otherness. The one who is concerned about either the Decree of Heaven or the Will of God is not egocentric. In this sense, he is more mature than the one who does not care about them.

Self-cultivation leads one to live in accord with the Decree of Heaven without making mistakes against what is right. The Decree of Heaven is so integrated into one's character that there is no dichotomy between one's desire and what is to be desired. In Chinese philosophy, the sage is always the one who, to a supreme degree, synthesizes in himself all the antitheses.[15] He has "sageliness within and kingliness without." We may well say that the sage is a being who is integrated and harmonious.

With internal integration and harmony, the superior man is able to endure tension and frustration. This inner strength was evident in the life of Confucius; he endured the agony of poverty, unemployment, and rejection. Traveling with his disciples under the most deprived circumstances, he showed a remarkable degree of inner composure in continuing his teaching, while his disciples could not take it. Tzu-lu, one of his eminent followers, asked, "Must a superior man also endure privation?" To this, Confucius replied: "A superior man stands firm in his misery. It is the inferior man who gives way to license in times of trouble." [16] Without internal integration and harmony, it would have been impossible for him to go through his later years of wandering.

We find a similar emphasis in Mencius' thought. When one is in trouble, he is often encouraged to meditate on what he said. For Mencius, the great man is the one who takes his place in the seat of rectitude and pursues the Great Way of the world. When he succeeds, he shares his success with the common people; when he fails, he pursues his principles in solitude. The great man is the one whose character cannot be tainted or bent by the riches and honors of this world.[17] The great man has not only the strength to stand firmly in facing poverty but also the strength to overcome the temptation of honor, prestige, and riches. History shows that both in the East and in the West great men always have inner strength. They are often persecuted, put into prison, or exiled because of their radical views. To endure suffering seems to be the lot of great men. Mencius observed:

> When the Heaven is about to bestow great responsibility on any man, it will train his mind with suffering, his sinews and bones with hard work, his body with hunger; it will put him to poverty, place obstacles in the paths of his doing, so as to make his mind alert, harden his character, and improve whatever is incompetent.[18]

Unless one is internally integrated, he cannot have the inner strength to cope with the manifold difficulties in life. This inner strength is achieved through a long period of self-cultivation.

Christians may say that their strength to cope with hardships, difficulties, and deprivations comes from the presence of the Spirit. But one of the characteristics of both Christian maturity and Confucian maturity is the possession of this strength to sustain tension and frustrations, which is also the characteristic of psychological maturity. For the pragmatic modern men, to possess this strength is primary and how to interpret it is secondary.

## 2. HUMAN-HEARTEDNESS (*JEN*) AND SOCIAL HARMONY

Besides self-cultivation, another aspect of Confucian maturity centers around "ordering and harmonizing the world." This is the social emphasis of Confucian thought. It concerns the interpersonal relationships between ruler and minister, father and son, husband and wife, elder brother and younger brother, and friends. From the Confucian point of view, no one is isolated or unrelated. No one lives in a vacuum. To be a man is to be related to other human beings. This is the nature of man, for man is a social being. His self-cultivation is not only to integrate himself internally but also to order and harmonize the world externally. Man's social nature is well expressed by the structure of the Chinese character for "man," *jen,* which consists of two strokes. It is significant that "marriage" is often described as "becoming a man" (*ch'eng jen*) like the two strokes coming together to form the word "man" (*jen*). A single person is not fully human from this point of view. He is only half human and is in need of union with his other half. Another Chinese character with the same pronunciation, *jen* (human-heartedness), consists of the word "man" and the word "two." This word *jen* may be translated in several ways. Lin Yu-t'ang translates it as "true manhood"; Hugh and Bodde, as "human-heartedness"; Wing-tsit Chan, as "humanity." The two Chinese *jen* words are closely related and are sometimes equated in signifying that the one who is man is the human-hearted one.

True human-heartedness consists of two persons. A single man or woman does not fulfill true human nature, because true personhood is fully manifested only in interpersonal relationships. True humanity cannot be realized in total isolation from other human beings. Therefore, the mature man is the man of human-heartedness in harmony with others, whether they be ruler or minister, husband or wife, father or son, elder brother or younger brother, or simply friends. From the Confucian point of view, it is inconceivable to meet a stranger or to have an enemy. However, in fact they exist.

The essence of human-heartedness is love. The word *jen* is often used in connection with the word *ai* (love), which includes both agape love and eros love. Confucius said, "*Jen* (human-heartedness) consists in loving others." [19] Without love, there is no true personhood. Hostility would destroy humanity. One's maturity is measured by how much he is able to love others. Whether one is the superior man or the inferior man is determined by his ability to establish a loving relationship with other persons. "The inferior man often gets into trouble because of his love for talking, but the superior man often gets into trouble because of his love for the people." [20] This shows that love characterizes the life of the superior man.

The superior man is not the egoistic, selfish man. He is not primarily concerned with himself. The man of human-heartedness is considerate toward others. He is the "one who, in seeking to establish himself, finds a foothold for others, and who, desiring attainment for himself, first helps others to attain." [21] But this love for others does not exclude the other aspect of love, namely, self-love; for true love does not include masochistic sacrifice. The direction of human-heartedness is to take one's own feeling as guidance in dealing with others. Empathy and identification are needed for the practice of human-heartedness. Positively, one should do to others what he wishes for himself. Negatively, one should not do to others what he does not wish for himself. One who truly loves others does not neglect his social duties. If he does, his love would be untrue. The one who really loves others is the one who is able to perform his social duties properly. He does not justify his negligence of public duties by his preoccupation with private matters.

From the text, "Clever words and flattering looks seldom speak of human-heartedness," [22] we can see the close relationship between human-heartedness (*jen*) and sincerity (*ch'eng*) in Confucian thought. True human-heartedness is sincere. Clever words and flattering looks are the expressions of hypocrisy, dishonesty, and deceitfulness. Those persons who make use of clever words and flattering looks in dealing with other people are likely to be regarded as hypocrites. Hypocrites are internally disintegrated. They do not have integrity. They cannot be sincere to others, because they are not sincere to themselves. They do not have the courage to be themselves; therefore, they do not have the courage to say what they want to say from their hearts. They pretend to be more than they are. Like Jesus, Confucius was critical of hypocrisy. A harmonious interpersonal relationship cannot be established by clever words and flattering looks, though the skillful pretender may succeed temporarily. Without internal integration, there can be no external harmony. Therefore, we can see that Confucian human-heartedness (*jen*) is also based on self-acceptance and self-respect. The man of true human-heartedness is the man of "productive-orientation" in Erich Fromm's sense. He does not relate to others superficially by means of pretension and deceitfulness, because he cannot allow himself to be alienated from his true being. He refuses to use clever words and flattering looks, because these are destructive to his own integrity as well as to the integrity of others. He extends himself and participates whole-heartedly in causes outside himself for the welfare of his fellow human beings. He is passionately involved in the struggle of the oppressed instead of being a mere spectator who is afraid to make any decisive commitment.

Human-heartedness is not something unreachable, abstract, or impractical. Confucius said: "Is *jen* far away? I desire for *jen*, and behold, it is right there at hand." [23] It is shown in relationships with parents, marriage partner, children, brothers, and sisters, for "filial piety and brotherly respect are the root of *jen*." [24] In the actual practice of human-heartedness, the family is the starting point from which one moves out into society and the world. "When the personhood is cultivated, the household will be regulated; when the household is regulated, the state will be in order; and when the state is in order, there will be peace throughout the world." [25] True manhood is not expressed arbitrarily without concern for the harmony of society. It is believed that internal integration achieved through self-cultivation leads to external harmony manifested in the happy life of the family, the orderliness of the state, and the peace of the world.

The concept of human-heartedness (*jen*) was further developed by Mencius and others. In *The Book of Mencius, jen* is synonymous with "man's mind," and we read that "the man of *jen* loves others." [26] Because of Mencius' strong emphasis on the goodness of human nature, he believes that man has a "mind which cannot bear to see the suffering of others, . . . the feeling of commiseration." [27] Man, by his very nature, has the feeling of shame, the feeling of modesty, and the sense of right and wrong. Mencius attacked the egoism of Yang Chu, whose main principle is that of "each one for himself." At the same time, he opposed the universal love of Mo Tzu, which is a kind of unlimited all-embracing love. He said: "The superior man, in his relation to things, loves them but does not have the feeling of human-heartedness. In his relation to people, he has human-heartedness but no deep feeling of family affection." [28]

What is inherent in man is not Mo Tzu's kind of

unlimited universal love. Rather, it is the feeling of being unable to bear the suffering of others. This feeling was well expressed in the story of Yü, a sage in ancient legend who subdued the primeval flood. Yü felt that if anyone were drowned, it was as if he himself were being drowned. Yet this story points out that the human-heartedness inherent in man has developed through a long period of self-cultivation. It is manifested in this feeling of commiseration. It is a kind of empathy for fellowmen which is almost mystical.[29] Unlike the Confucianists, who considered human-heartedness as something naturally developed from within human nature, Mo Tzu and his followers considered all-embracing indiscriminatory love as something ascetically added to man. For the Confucianists the practice of human-heartedness is for its own sake, whereas for the Mohists the practice of all-embracing love is for a utilitarian purpose. The Confucianists are inner-directed. According to Mencius and later Confucianists, the king (*wang*) is a sage who is virtuous. Unlike the military lord (*pa*) who sets the state in order by physical force, the sage-king's power is moral virtue by which he gains followers in the same way that Confucius won his disciples.[30]

According to Confucianism, the practice of human-heartedness is based on the kind of relationship one has with the person. Consequently, there should be differences in the degree of love one gives and receives. A Confucianist would love his parents more than the men of his clan; he would love the members of his own clan more than the men of his district; he would love the members of his own district more than those in his own state; and he would love the members of his own state more than the men of a nearby state. Furthermore, one would love people more than things. The Confucianist considered it proper that men do not love their neighbors' children in the same way as they love their brothers' children. However, Mencius encouraged his disciples to extend the treatment they gave to the aged in their families to the aged in other people's families and the treatment they gave to the young in their own families to the young in other people's families.[31] It is desirable to extend one's scope of activity to include others instead of being tightly closed to oneself. This extension is similar to what Gordon W. Allport considers a characteristic of a mature person—"the extension of the self." There is a certain degree of empathy and identification with external love objects, which both Confucius and Mencius would uphold as a sign of maturity through self-cultivation. It is not inwardly directed; rather, it is outwardly directed. It seeks external integration and harmony.

In the history of Chinese philosophy, no other concept has gone through so many phases of development as human-heartedness (*jen*). Prior to Confucius, *jen* was merely a specific virtue of benevolence. Confucius turned it into the universal virtue and basis of all goodness. Later, his grandson Tzu Ssu developed it to include metaphysical implications.[32] The Han (206 B.C.–A.D. 220) scholars interpreted it as love, affection, and "people living together." Han Yü (768–824) interpreted it as universal love. The Neo-Confucianists of the Sung dynasty (960–1279) interpreted it variously as impartiality, consciousness, unity with heaven and earth, the character of love and the principle of mind, the power of production and reproduction, seeds that generate virtue, and so on. In translating *The Analects* into German, Richard Wilhelm used the words *Liebe* ("love") and *Sittlichkeit* ("morality") for the word *jen*;[33] and K'ang Yu-wei (1858–1927), who tried to synthesize Western science and Confucianism, described *jen* as ether and electricity, which is all-pervasive.

Besides his new interpretation of *jen* in natural scientific terms, K'ang envisioned the coming of the Age of Great Peace and Unity, a utopia for social reform. Stressing the present social reform, he boldly dismissed the age-old Confucian idols of sage-kings who represented perfection and were to be imitated. He propounded his novel concept of historical progress through three stages toward utopia. The theory of three ages was not new. In his commentary on a passage in the Confucian Classics, *The Book of Rites,* he traced his theory to Confucius, who was said to have taught that history progresses from the Age of Chaos to that of Small Peace, and eventually to that of Great Peace and Unity. K'ang's utopia is spelled out in detail as an ideal state of nondistinctions between states, races, classes, sexes, families, occupations, species, physical forms, and so on. Therefore, in the Age of Great Peace and Unity, there are no emperors, kings, rulers, elders, official titles, or ranks; there are no husbands and wives, no quarrels over women, no necessity for adultery, suppression of sex desires, complaint, hatred, divorce, kidnap, or murder; and there is no private property, no litigation over land, residence, industrial or business property, no tax, customs, conscription, no crime of cheating or desertion. The whole world becomes a great unity and all people are equal. Since man's nature is good and his ability and intelligence is superior, new institutions appear every day and public benefits increase daily and in every way. The people of the whole world reach the realm of humanity, longevity, perfect happiness, infinite goodness and wisdom. All people live in public dwellings and there is no difference in dress between men and women; people will think only of immortality on earth. His ideas were so radical that his book *Ta-t'ung shu* (Book of Great Unity) was kept unpublished until 1935, eight years after his death. The philosophical bases for his utopia are two: (1) his theory of historical progress and evolution and (2) his interpretation of *jen* which is the power unifying all people as one and permeating everywhere like ether and electricity. The gradual extension of love for parents will reach all men because *jen* is the power of attraction based on the "feeling of the same kind." Thus, *jen* becomes universal love. But individuals exist as individuals even in this world of harmony. According to K'ang, Confucius was born in the Age of Disorder, we are in the Age of Rising Peace, and there will be the Age of Great Unity.

Is Confucian *jen* different from Christian love? This question has attracted wide attention among Chinese Christians as well as Westerners. They tend to emphasize Christian love as sacrificial agape love, which is indiscriminative, universal, and all-embracing like Mo Tzu's Universal Love, whereas Confucian love is discriminative in accordance with the nature of relationships with the person to be loved. Often it is asserted that Confucian love is selfish, while Christian love is unselfish. Confucian love is eros, which is inferior to Christian agape. Therefore, Confucianists should learn from Christians, and their "*eros* must be transformed to *agape*." [34] As discussed in Chapter III, the separation of eros and agape is artificial and conceptual. In fact, both are integrated and inseparable. There is a legitimate self-love which is not egoism, the self-love which is implied in "Love your neighbor as yourself." God is love (*agapē*) in Christianity. If there is no legitimate self-love being integrated in agape, there will be no justification for God to reveal to men that he is love and that men should love him. How could it be that the self-giving God sent his only Son, Jesus Christ, in human form asking his disciples to love him if there is no self-love in his agape? The god who asserts himself as agape and openly demands that men should love him with all their hearts and minds is a liar, a hypocrite, a tyrant, and a dictator if there is no legitimate self-love to which he appeals. Christian love is paradoxical in nature; self-giving is self-fulfilling: he who gives his life shall find it. This paradox presupposes two diametrically opposed polarities, self-giving and self-loving, but they are integrated. The self-love in agape is the basis for righteousness and justice, which is inseparable from

God's grace, forgiveness, and mercy. This self-love is the basis for just self-defense. Likewise, this self-love is the basis of distinction, discrimination, and differentiation. This self-love is the link between Christian agape and Confucian *jen*. Furthermore, both are self-giving, other-directed love object, seeking to reach all men ultimately. Self-love is not selfish love. Selfish love is greedy, egoistic, dominating, invasive, expansive, and aggressive, whereas self-love knows its boundary and is bound by justice. Self-love is the source of internal integration, whereas self-giving love is the source of external integration and harmony. Both are interrelated and integrated.

Confucian philosophy is a social philosophy. It aims not only at the internal integration of each individual but also at the external harmony of society. Besides the "rectification of the mind," Confucius propounded "the rectification of names" (*cheng ming*), which is well summarized in these words: "Let the ruler be ruler, the minister be minister, the father be father, and the son be son." [35] There should be no discrepancy between names and actualities. Each name implies its unique role and quality in social and family relationships. Everyone should perform the duties that his titles require. Without this correspondence between names and actualities, there can be no harmonious relationships. In *The Book of Mencius,* proper human relationships were defined: "between father and son, affection; between ruler and minister, righteousness; between husband and wife, separate roles; between old and young, proper order; between friends, faithfulness." [36] These are important guides for harmonious relationships in the family and society.

From the Confucian point of view, the basic human relationship is that of father and son. That is why filial piety is so fundamental in the practice of human-heartedness (*jen*). The Chinese character for filial piety (*hsiao*) is structured to suggest an old man supported by his son. This support is not legalistic duty, but an affectionate gesture. In feudal society, men were considered to be superior to women, and the husband was the head. The role of husband was that of being responsible for all matters outside the family, whereas the wife's role was inside the family. Friendships were honored. James Legge, well known for his translation of the Chinese Classics into English, remarked that he did not know any other scheme of society that gave as much prominence to friendship as Confucian society.[37] Faithfulness is the basis for sound friendship, which is person-centered instead of profit-centered.

In seeking to order and harmonize the state and the world, Confucius insisted that all people should be ruled by the *li* (rituals, ceremonies, rules of conduct, mores, and so on) and morality, and not by laws, punishments, or any form of coercion. In the feudal society of the early Chou dynasty, the aristocrats, who were known as *chün tzu*, were governed by the *li*, whereas the ordinary people, who were known as *hsiao jen*, were governed by punishments (*hsing*). Confucius was revolutionary in insisting that both the aristocrats and the ordinary people were equally governed by the *li*. He was opposed to Han Fei Tzu and other Legalists who were in favor of absolute social control by punishments because men were completely evil. In the Confucian way of thinking, social harmony is achieved through the self-cultivation of each individual in attaining the sagehood of the ancient period of perfection. Even Hsün Tzu, whose view of man's nature was pessimistic, agreed that man possesses intelligence which makes it possible for him to become good. He argued that man could become a Yü, a traditional sage, because of man's original intelligence. Even the man on the street has the capacity of knowing human-heartedness and righteousness for virtuous living. The humanity in each individual is as much a reality as mankind. The power that can assure the order and harmony of the state and the world lies in internal self-cultivation, and not in laws and punishments by the rulers.

Self-cultivation leads one not only to social harmony in human relationships in the family and society but also to moral and spiritual unity with the universe. In the autobiographical statement of Confucius, we find that at the age of fifty, Confucius was said to know the Decree of Heaven (*t'ien ming*), a discernment and discovery of one's destiny in history. In *The Book of Mencius*, the universe is considered to be essentially moral, and the understanding of this moral universe is called "knowing heaven." One who knows heaven is a citizen of heaven (*t'ien min*).[38] By the full development of the moral nature which is inherent in man ("All things are complete within us"), not only can one know heaven—one can also become one with heaven. By the practice of human-heartedness (*jen*), one becomes less egoistic and selfish, and eventually the distinction between oneself and the rest of the world disappears completely, so that he becomes identified with the universe as a whole. This state of spiritual cultivation is difficult to describe, even by Mencius himself. It is supremely great and strong, and one feels the moving power which pervades all. It is the Great Morale (*hao jan chih ch'i*) which makes one identify himself with the universe by the long accumulation of righteousness and the understanding of truth (*Tao*). If one constantly practices human-heartedness and righteousness, the Great Morale will emerge from the very center of one's being.

Is there anything comparable to this in Christianity? The basic assumption in Christianity is that man is a sinner in need of divine grace by which he is reconciled to God, to himself, to others, and to the whole universe. Self-cultivation is impossible because man is evil. He needs to be transformed completely by the Spirit. This is diametrically opposed to Confucian self-cultivation. But whether the inherent goodness, the human-heartedness (*jen*) in man, is purely human and natural (Confucian) or the presence of the divine Spirit (Christian) is hard to determine. From the Christian point of view, the divine Spirit also works among nonbelievers, including Confucianists. The Confucian self-cultivation is worked out by oneself, whereas Christian reconciliation depends on the divine Spirit. But both are subjective inner experiences of integration and harmony resulting in external harmony with other human beings and the whole universe. Both work against egoism and selfishness.

Finally, it may well be worth our effort to examine the life experiences of some of those who have been exposed to both Confucianism and Christianity. Conflicts often arise between one's Christian obedience to God and his filial piety to the parents. But these conflicts can be solved if one is convinced of the integration between his love for God and his love for men. A widely known Chinese scholar who is now in his late eighties said in an interview about maturity, "If Jesus were here today, and if Confucius were here also, they would become good friends." They could be good friends, it seems to me, because of their common concern for the centrality of the father-son relationship in their teaching: Jesus Christ teaches the Fatherhood of God; Confucius teaches filial piety. Psychologically, the emotional life of the individual as infant and child determines the kind of religion that he or she can respond to and make his or her own. One's father image has great influence on his understanding and acceptance of the Fatherhood of God. When the infant encounters love he encounters God. God is in that parental love as well as parents. Filial piety is significant to the understanding and acceptance of God in this respect. Experientially, Confucianism prepares the way to Christianity and expresses it concretely in human relationships.

# V

# Taoist Maturity

ANOTHER MAINSTREAM of thought in Chinese culture is Taoism, which is quite different from Confucianism. In English, Taoism can mean either a religion or a philosophy. In Chinese, the religion is called Tao chiao, the philosophy, Tao chia. In this chapter, our main purpose is to discuss the concept of maturity in philosophical Taoism, which has shaped the character and life of the Chinese as strongly as Confucianism yet in different ways and at particular times for over two thousand years. Though it has been absorbed into Chinese Buddhism and Neo-Confucianism and no longer exists as an independent philosophical school, Taoism and its immanent power and validity cannot be ignored. In the words of a modern Chinese philosopher: "Taoist philosophy is not dead. One finds it everywhere, for it is tightly woven into the fabric of Chinese life." [1] Chinese blood contains the consciousness and feeling of the Taoists, and it is difficult for foreigners to understand Chinese traditions and character without a knowledge of Taoism.[2] It is even difficult for the Chinese to understand themselves without such knowledge. Like Confucianism, Taoism was conceived and developed by the Chinese mind in the massive agricultural land of the Middle Kingdom. The two systems of thought grew together like twins in the family, who encounter each other daily.

While Confucius was traveling from state to state, he and his disciples met many recluses who ridiculed him for his vain efforts to save the world. They described him as "the one who knows he cannot succeed, yet keeps on trying." [3] These recluses were individualists who detached themselves from the world and sought to maintain their personal purity without making any effort to change the "swelling torrent." They lived in the world of nature. The Taoists, however, were not of this type. On the contrary, they retired in seclusion from the world in order to work out a system of thought that would give meaning to life and justify their action. The earliest exponent was Yang Chu, whose ideas were: "Each one for himself" and "the despising of things and valuing of life." [4] The greatest Taoist in Chinese history was Lao Tzu. Later on, Chuang Tzu developed his ideas metaphysically.

Lao Tzu can mean two things: Lao Tzu the person, and *Lao Tzu* the book, which is also called *Tao Te Ching* (Classic of the Way and Its Power). Chinese tradition regards Lao Tzu as being about twenty years older than Confucius. In the 1920's and 1930's many Chinese and Western scholars rejected this view and dated him about the fourth or third century B.C., but since then the tendency has been to accept the tradition. The theory that Lao Tzu never existed or is merely a legend is no longer seriously entertained. Traditionally, Lao Tzu has been known as a native of the state of Ch'u (in the southern part of Honan Province today). Lao Tzu literally means the "Old Master." His last name was Li, his first name Er, and his posthumous name Tan. He became a custodian of the imperial archives at the royal court of the Chou dynasty. Confucius once visited him to obtain information on rites and ceremonies. Finally, he abandoned the royal court and departed westward. At the request of a gatekeeper he wrote his treatise on *The Way (Tao) and Its Power*. Later Taoist propagandists, competing for prestige with Buddhists, claimed that Lao Tzu traveled to India and converted the Buddha himself to Taoism.

The book of Lao Tzu is the most frequently translated

of all Chinese texts. It is also the most obscure and
diversified in interpretation, and there are more commentaries on it than on any other Chinese classic.[5] It consists
of from 5,227 to 5,722 words, depending on the edition,
and is often called the Five Thousand Characters Classic.
Modern scholarship admits knowing nothing with cer-
tainty about its author or authors, and it is possible that
the book entitled *Lao Tzu* was the work of several writers
containing a few sayings of the original Lao Tzu. The
materials chosen are often terse, aphoristic, cryptic, and
rhymed. It contains no dialogue, no historical event, no
proper noun. Yet we can find in it the wisdom and
thought-treasure of the Old Master whom Confucius
visited and of whom he said to his disciples on his return,
"This day, I have seen Lao Tzu and he is a dragon."
Through the wisdom of this "dragon" and the mystical
insight of the imaginative poet Chuang Tzu, we can find
the answer to the question of Taoist maturity, sagehood,
and ultimate ideals. We know little about Chuang Tzu's
life except that he was a contemporary of Mencius, that
he was a native of the state of Meng on the border
between the modern Shantung and Honan provinces, that
he was famous for his writings and ideas. On being asked
by King Wei of Ch'u to be a state minister, he flatly turned
down the offer. Just as Mencius did not merely expound
the ideas of Confucius but also added something of his
own, Chuang Tzu definitely made the differences between
Confucianism and Taoism sharper and advanced his
transcendental mysticism beyond Lao Tzu.

## 1. EGO-LESS SELFHOOD
### AND INTEGRATION

Taoism is almost diametrically opposed to Confucianism. This may seem to imply that Taoism does not
emphasize self-cultivation, which is so essential in Confucian maturity. But, in fact, Taoism has its self-cultivation

which is methodologically contradictory to that of Confucian maturity. Taoist self-cultivation is a negative type in contrast to Confucian positive cultivation. Nevertheless, the ultimate purpose is similar; each aims at internal integration and harmony.

Taoism is a severe critic of Confucianism by opposing the Confucian conformity with its nonconformity. Confucius was known as "the one who knows he cannot succeed, yet keeps on trying." [6] In contrast, Lao Tzu was such a quiet pacifist that he advocated the unconventional way of nondesire (*wu yü*) and nonaction (*wu wei*). Instead of extending knowledge through the investigation of things, Lao Tzu taught the way of unlearning what one has learned in achieving internal integration and harmony. Instead of strengthening one's willpower, Lao Tzu seemed to propose the weakening of one's willpower by self-contentment and self-acceptance, which puts ego-striving at rest. If one does not have desire, there will be no inner conflicts. For a man of nondesire, egoism has lost its sting. Taoist self-cultivation leads to ego-less selfhood, which is the center of Taoist maturity. [7]

The Taoist sage is not egoistic. Lao Tzu proposed not to exalt the worthy so that there will be no competition, not to value rare treasures so that there will be no stealing, not to display objects of desire so that the people's hearts shall not be disturbed. [8] He advised the people: "Be yourself, Embrace simplicity, Reduce selfishness, and Have few desires." [9] If all men are free of desires, the world will be at peace of its own accord. The mature Taoist has no desire to defend himself from humiliation or underestimation by others, because he has conquered himself and therefore is truly strong. [10] He is not irritated when others do not recognize his importance. Nor does he expect others to accept his eminence, for he is satisfied with his own self-estimation. He does not exalt himself, for he accepts himself for what he is. He who accepts himself for what he is is always contented. [11] His ego-less selfhood is analogous to "satisfied selfhood" or "desire-less selfhood." There is no greater disaster than discon-tentment. Thus Taoist self-cultivation strives to reduce one's own desires. This is comparable to the Christian teaching that one should "rejoice always" and "give thanks in all circumstances" (I Thess. 5:16, 18). Thanks-giving is a great virtue from the Christian point of view. Christian thanksgiving implies the personal God to whom one gives thanks and something for which he is thankful, always being in dialogue with the ultimate Personality. Taoist self-contentment is so introverted and isolationis-tic that one tends to cut ties with the external reality and become a hermit. One critic has said, "The good Taoist is a dead man." Nevertheless, psychologically both signify a state of internal integration and harmony, a state of self-acceptance. "Ego-less selfhood" is internally inte-grated.

One may think that Taoist nondesire is self-destructive, like self-hatred. "The sage desires to have no desire" [12] does not mean that he wants to be in the state of a dead man. The dead man does not desire at all. The Taoist sage is in a paradoxical state. His desire "to have no desire" is comparable to the paradox in Christian matu-rity, "He who loves his life loses it, and he who hates his life in this world will keep it for eternal life" (John 12:25). This paradox is basically the paradox in psychological maturity, the paradox between self-love and love for others—the most selfish man has least love for others, and the man who loves others most loves himself most, because self-love and love for others are identical and inseparable. On the other hand, the man who hates others hates himself.

The principle of ego-less selfhood was deemed to be applicable also to political and social affairs. The Taoist ruler keeps the hearts of his people vacuous (*hsü*), weakens their ambitions, and causes them to be without knowledge and desire.[13] He would let the people retain the virtues of simplicity and unselfishness as well as the virtue of few desires. This is contrary to the ideas that apathy is evil and that we should motivate the apathetic by reinforcements, rewards, and punishments. The Taoist does not advise the young by saying, "Boys! Be ambitious!" The only advice he can give is to have few desires, to be simple, unselfish, and vacuous. If the Taoist makes use of modern motivational theory, he tends to use it in discouraging the process of civilization, in reducing the elaboration of social rules and regulations, and in stopping the materialistic improvement of living conditions because he idealizes simple rural society.

In a society that advocates free competition, everyone wants to climb the social ladder so that he can assume leadership in his local community, professional organization, and religious institution. But this is not the Taoist ideal. Instead of striving for leadership and supremacy, the Taoists are those whose existence is merely known.[14] One may deem the Taoist way of ruling a kind of ancient colonialism which suppresses all desires for improvement and advancement. But this is not so. The point is that the ruler does not deliberately intend to exploit his people by making them desireless and self-content, lest they should rebel against him. This simple rural society is what he believes to be the ideal. The ruler himself tries to be desireless and self-content. He himself finds his place in the background and is satisfied with it. He teaches his people humility, and the people see him practice humility himself. In Taoism, humility is symbolized by water, and the Taoist sage is like water, which "is good, for it benefits all things and does not compete with them, and is also content with the places that all despise." [15] He never strives for the great place of leadership, but his greatness is acknowledged. He has no desires, but the people themselves become simple.[16]

In the teachings of Confucius, the practice of human-heartedness (*jen*) makes one overcome egoism and re-

spond with propriety (*li*). Mencius attacked the egoism of
Yang Chu, who was known for his doctrine of self-
preservation to the point of not even plucking out a single
hair, even if he could benefit the entire world by doing
so.[17] Taoism developed from the phase of Yang Chu's
egoistic self-preservation to that of Lao Tzu's "ego-less
selfhood." In the philosophy of Lao Tzu, egoism is out of
place because egoism is the root of human suffering and
the source of internal disintegration and external disharmony. Egoism leads to strife and competition. For the
winner, competition brings thrill, excitement, and satisfaction. But for the defeated, it offers despair and mental
anguish. In a highly competitive society, Taoism seems
irrelevant because it encourages withdrawal from society
and its manifold competitions.

Taoism is a philosophy for the minority. It is a means
to internal integration and harmony for those who are
doomed to be defeated. But this is not entirely so. Every
Chinese would find Taoism as appealing as Confucianism
at one time or another in his or her life. It is not
appropriate to call Taoism a philosophy of dropouts or
defeatists because of its emphasis on simplicity, unselfishness, and few desires. Rather, it is a philosophy of
a historian who served as a custodian of imperial archives
in the ancient times when the society disintegrated and all
forms of government seemed useless. Lao Tzu was
ultimately this-worldly and socially-minded though his
social theory was unconventional and radical. After a
long period of reflection, he came to see that "the sage
only smiles like an amused child and treats his people all
as children." [18] A smile is an expression of one's internal
harmony. This is what the Taoist sage has achieved. No
matter who wins the battle, the internal battle is over and
there is inner peace. There is no more ego-striving or
selfish desire within him.

Confucian self-cultivation emphasizes the extension of
knowledge through the investigation of things, but Taoist
self-cultivation is to have few desires, to be simple, and to

be natural. It is to undo all the artificialities of human civilization and to return to the natural simplicity which is well symbolized by the "Uncarved Block" (*p'u*). It is to return to spontaneity (*chu jan*), a state of complete harmony within and without, in which one's ego-striving ceases to exist. The Taoists criticized Confucian virtues such as human-heartedness (*jen*), righteousness (*yi*), and propriety (*li*) and regarded them as artificial human inventions. By abandoning Confucian wisdom, by discarding human-heartedness and righteousness, and by forsaking skills and profits, the people would return to true filial piety and deep love, and there would be no theft or robbery.[19] Virtues, skills, and profits are created to satisfy human desires. If ego-striving ceases to exist, there would be no need for the propagation of virtues. The Taoists see the important issues of modern civilization, human rebellion against its artificiality, dehumanization through machinization and industrial technology, urbanization, and bureaucracy.

## 2. THE WAY (*TAO*), NONACTION (*WU WEI*), AND HARMONY

The psychologically mature person is characterized by his reality perception; he sees his true self and gains an accurate picture of his external environment. His perception is not distorted by his emotional needs. The mature Christian knows his own true self, his own limitations as well as potentialities; he knows his place in the total scheme of things. The mature Confucianist knows his own true self also; he knows what he knows, and knows what he does not know; he knows his own destiny, the Decree of Heaven as well as social propriety. Likewise, the mature Taoist perceives himself accurately. Lao Tzu says,

> To know what you do not know is to have genuine knowledge, and to pretend to know what you do not know is to be deluded.[20]

Reality perception in Taoism is not only about one's true self but also about knowing the most essential, the most fundamental, the roots of all things, namely, the Tao (Way). It is to know the Truth of all truths, the Principle underlying all principles, the Form behind all forms, the Nature of nature, the Nameless behind all names, the One, the Ultimate One. It is to know the Non-being behind all beings, the Undifferentiated Oneness behind all differentiated existences, the Simple behind all complexities. It is to know the Way (*Tao*) which is the Invisible, the Inaudible, and the Subtle. The Tao is often symbolized by Water, Female, and Infant.

The Tao is elusive and vague.[21] It is beyond description. All things are nameable, but the Tao is unnameable. Lao Tzu begins his discourse in these words:

> The Tao that can be stated is not the everlasting Tao; the Name that can be named is not the everlasting name. The unnamable is the origin of Heaven and Earth; the namable is the mother of all things.[22]

The Tao is eternal, everlasting, and cannot be articulated or explained. It is that by which anything and everything has come to be. It is undifferentiated and yet perfect. It preexisted heaven and earth. It does not depend on anything, nor does it change. It is operative everywhere and yet is free from danger. It may be thought to be the mother of the universe. It moves everywhere, left or right. It consummates its work and yet does not demand credit for it. It provides clothing and food for all and yet does not demand to be their master. It may be called the Small, for it is always desireless. It may be called the Great, for all things come to it. It is imperceptible, inexhaustible.[23]

The Taoist sage is one who knows the Tao, and to know the Tao is to follow the Tao. He "who follows the Tao identifies himself with the Tao."[24] He who identifies himself with the Tao practices the Way of nonaction (*wu wei*), for the "reversion is the action of Tao." [25] This reversion can be seen from the fact that "the Tao which is bright appears to be dark; the Tao which goes forward seems to fall back; the Tao which is even appears uneven.[26] This reversion is also illustrated by the fact that the Taoist sage is as "pointed as a square, but does not pierce; he is as sharp as a knife, but does not cut; he is as straight as an unbent line, but does not extend; he is as bright as light, but does not dazzle." [27] The Taoist sage teaches by what he is rather than by what he says. He admits his inferiority, and thereby he becomes superior and the leader of all. In order to be ahead of the people, he follows them. Thus, even if he places himself above the people, they do not feel his weight; and even if he places himself in front of the people, they do no harm to him.[28]

The Taoist sage does not brag or boast. He is humble because he knows well that when humility is replaced by pride and arrogance, he is doomed to fail because this is against the Tao. He does not intimidate others by his authority, nor does he compel them by force. He functions like water flowing to the place that nobody wants. His strength is in his weakness. The Tao is the model of sagehood and is the standard of all men. The Taoist sage yields himself as if he is as weak as a female and as flexible as water, but "genuine yielding can be like a masochist red flag to a sadist bull." [29] Nonaction (*wu wei*) does not mean to be "dry wood and dead ashes." It is a subtle form of action.

The Taoist sees the strength of weakness, the greatness of smallness, the usefulness of uselessness, and the loudness of silence. He sees the effectiveness of nonverbal communication and the aggressiveness of nonaggression. He is convinced that humility and compassion can work like gravity in interpersonal relationships. Like Confucianists, Taoists advocate the power of morality and virtue in opposition to violence. Power, violence, and oppression are only temporary means of controlling people; they do not last for long. Man intuitively senses the feelings of another man and responds to his attitude rather than to what he does or what he says. His maturity is manifested in his perception of how the Tao works in the universe.

It is by no means accidental that the Greek word *logos* in the Prologue of The Gospel According to John was translated as *Tao* in the Chinese Bible. The historical person Jesus of Nazareth was the Tao Incarnate. His life embodied the power of love and exemplified the nobility of lowliness and humility, the strength of weakness, and the wisdom of foolishness. He rejected violence and showed the Way of true power which did not reside in swords, spears, and other weapons of the Roman Empire. This Great Tao flows everywhere, but only the mature have ears to hear and eyes to see the Way manifesting itself in the course of human history, and then become convinced that this is the Way. On the other hand, Tao has been translated as "Principle," "Creative Principle," or "Truth," not as abstract truth but as "Concrete Truth," or even as "divine intelligence of the universe." [30] Tao is the indigenous Chinese concept of ultimate reality which is close to the Christian concept of God in the sense that both are the origin of all things and epitomize the concept of maturity for men to emulate. But Tao is impersonal, whereas the Christian God is personal. Tao is natural, whereas God is both natural and supernatural. Tao is in the world, whereas God is in the world and transcends the world as well. The impersonal Tao has no will, memory, anxiety, forgiveness, foreknowledge, or afterthought, whereas the personal God has all aspects of a living personality. Unlike Confucianism whose concept of Tao is more objective, Lao Tzu considers Tao to be something from which we can never be separated. Tao is imminent in nature and is not far away from us.

The Tao is not only the Way of men, but also the Way

of nature. Joseph Needham, the renowned Cambridge sinologist who has made a monumental study of science and civilization in China, points out that "Tao brought all things into existence and governs their every action." He also sees nonaction (*wu wei*) from the point of view of nature and interprets it as "letting things work out their destinies in accordance with their intrinsic principles. To be able to practice *wu wei* implies learning from Nature by observations which are essentially scientific."[31] In this respect, the spirit of Taoism is scientific, but it does not advocate the conquest of nature and the exploitation of it by human inventions. It is inconceivable for the Taoist to explore the laws of nature in order to conquer nature and to exploit it to satisfy human egoistic desires. This is against the Tao. The purpose of discovering the Tao in nature is to be in harmony with nature. The tendency of this superscientific age is very much against the Tao, because man tries to become the master of nature rather than the co-worker with nature. To live comfortably in this world is to be friendly with nature instead of treating it as an enemy. There is a new proposal that we remake our natural world by giving back to it that which has been ruthlessly torn from it. Modern men are now awakened to their state of disharmony with nature and are determined to be co-workers rather than its ruthless exploiters.[32]

The basic Taoist principle is that "one should be in harmony with, not in rebellion against, the fundamental laws of the Universe."[33] This is the Taoist insight into the Way of human existence. This insight is now coming to modern men who have been treating nature as an enemy for so long. Albert Einstein was at all times firmly convinced of the harmony of the universe. He also firmly believed that men of different languages and of different political and cultural ideas should cooperate.[34] Furthermore, men should cooperate with nature. This is a sign of maturity. Increasingly, modern men seem ready to hear words of the Taoist sage: "To hasten the growth of life is ominous. To control the breath by the will is to overstrain it. To be overgrown is to decay. All this is against the Tao. And whatever is against the Tao soon ceases to exist." [35]

Man is not the master of nature and he will never be the master of this universe no matter how far human science and technology advance. This is the most bitter pill for man to swallow, but "that is the way it is." What troubles man most is his desire for supremacy, his thirst to conquer, to exploit, and to dominate, not only his own fellow human beings but also the nature which gives him resources for living. The "master race" psychology is an expression of this desire for supremacy, and there are countless manifestations of the same desire in our personal, institutional, national, and international relationships. What is to be controlled is man himself and his egoistic desire for supremacy. It makes man run against the Tao. The Taoists were the quietistic unconventionals and the unorthodox because of their uncommon insight into the fundamentals of things and reality. Their perception of reality is deep and penetrating. Lao Tzu's yearning for the simple, primitive, agricultural society is no longer relevant to modern technological metropolises, but his perception of the nature of things is surely relevant everywhere. His understanding of the way man and woman respond to each other is no less profound than that of experimental psychologists who draw their conclusions from animal behavior.

Mencius was democratic in advocating the right of the people to rebel against evil rulers. But Lao Tzu was even more democratic in perceiving the effectiveness of leadership from below, so that Hu Shih calls him a "rebel." [36] He saw the futility and vanity of legalistic rule in promulgating laws and supported the way of love and humility in the conquest of human hearts. Military conquest is not as secure as the winning of human hearts by compassion.

This is the way it works in interpersonal relationships. It is the way to do nothing which is unnatural, and the way to avoid aggression and violence.

*Wu wei* (nonaction) is neither an excuse for the lazy nor a magical trick for the Taoists to manipulate others indirectly and secretively in achieving their concealed desires. Lao Tzu is against any ulterior motive. He said, "The man of superior virtue takes no action, but has no ulterior motive to do so." [37] The Taoist practices nonaction because it is the way things are in nature and in human relationships. It is how the Tao functions. Otherwise, nonaction would become some kind of gimmick inherited from Lao Tzu. Then nonaction is no longer nonaction.

In nonaction (*wu wei*) we again find a paradox. It is the paradox of the effectiveness of nonaction, which is similar to that of nondesire (*wu yü*), Christian self-sacrifice, and of self-love and love for others. Nonaction is an action, a positive action in negative form, an activity in passive form. The key to turn the passive active and the negative positive is its acknowledgment and respect for the right of other fellow human beings and ultimately the right of the Way (*Tao*), the nature. The Taoist knows that unless he is in harmony with nature he will not survive for long. This harmony with nature is possible only if man recognizes the right of things in nature whose ultimate is the Way. This acknowledgment of the right of objective reality is akin to what Gordon W. Allport means by "self-objectification" and to antinarcissism in modern psychotherapy. It is the eradication of human egoism which is the sign of immaturity, sin, and mental illness and also the sign of "inferior man." This respect for the right of objective reality is positively manifested in the self-giving love for others in Christian maturity and the human-heartedness in Confucian maturity, whereas it is expressed negatively and introvertedly in Taoist maturity. In all cases, however, to be mature is to be less egoistic. Lao Tzu was very much concerned about social reform, but his negative approach makes Taoism introverted and individualistic. Furthermore, the ultimate reality Tao is impersonal in nature, so that Taoist maturity is lacking in warm interpersonal relationships, which characterize psychological maturity.

### 3. Transcendence and Wholeness (One)

In Paul Tillich's interpretation of the process of sanctification, self-transcendence is one of the four principles in determining the New Being. Likewise, Lewis J. Sherrill regards self-transcendence as one of the marks of the human self,[38] without particularly emphasizing it as the result of the presence of the Spirit. Self-transcendence means that man, who is in nature and subject to nature, is able to act and to transcend it simultaneously. This shows that man, who is physical, also dwells in the realm of spirit, which transcends the physical. This invaluable aspect of man prevents him from regarding himself as the helpless victim of the very laws and processes of physical nature that he has discovered. This aspect is particularly emphasized by Chuang Tzu, who speculated beyond this mundane world and became fanciful in his philosophy.

Chuang Tzu emphasized the basic teaching of Lao Tzu, but he developed his speculation in seeing the transcendent aspect of human nature. He made a distinction between what is "of man" and what is "of nature." What is "of man" is artificial and therefore evil. What is "of nature" is natural and therefore good. His ideal is to follow what is of nature. Happiness comes from following what is of nature; misery comes from following what is of man. Uniformity is achieved by man's effort in contradiction to what is natural. If things followed what is natural, there would be no uniformity. "The early sage did not make abilities and occupations uniform."[39] By nature, our abilities cannot be uniform. The abilities come from the Tao, and when they are fully and freely developed, they are the ideal. We are not supposed to lengthen the legs of the duck or to shorten the legs of the crane in order to make them equal for the achievement of uniformity, because this would be painful to the duck as well as to the crane.[40] This teaching is not much different from Lao Tzu's, for what makes Chuang Tzu distinctly unique is his emphasis on the transcendence of man in becoming identified with the Tao.

Chuang Tzu himself practiced this transcendence and took things from the transcendental point of view. This enabled him, when his wife died, to overcome his emotions and to accept her death as part of the natural process. He transcended his sorrow and stopped weeping. He was accused by his friend Hui Shih of being unkind to his wife, but he replied that although he was sad at first, after having examined the matter step by step he was able to see the whole process like the sequence of the four seasons, and that to go about weeping and wailing would be to proclaim himself ignorant of natural laws.[41] He was able to detach himself from his own predicament and see things objectively and transcendentally. This was a sign of his maturity.

This transcendence makes one see things as a whole, and it is the transcendence of all distinctions and differentiations that characterizes the Taoist sage. Chuang Tzu pointed out that "the perfect man has no self; the spiritual man has no achievement; and the true sage has no name." [42] Evidently, these terms—"the perfect man," "the spiritual man," and "the true sage"—are synonymous terms that indicate the ideal image of maturity. When one reaches this stage, he is no longer concerned about the distinction between "me" and "non-me" or "I" and "the rest of the world." He is no longer interested in parading his achievement or bragging about his greatness and supremacy. He is no longer obsessed with the question of whether or not his name is on the list or on the

front page of the newspaper. Names signify the differentiated state of being; when the undifferentiated wholeness
is differentiated, names are given. When a baby is born,
he is given a name. This reminds us of the words of Lao
Tzu: "The Sage embraces the One, and becomes a Pattern
of all under Heaven." [43] "One" is the undifferentiated
wholeness which is what the sage wants to embrace. It is
the most essential, the most fundamental, and the most
original. To achieve that state of transcending all distinctions and differentiations of this mundane world is to be
identified with the eternal Tao.

In one sense, this undifferentiated wholeness can be
compared to the primeval state of "without form and
void" prior to the creation in the first chapter of the book
of Genesis in the Bible, except that the Taoist "One" does
not carry the negative connotation of "darkness" which
was "upon the face of the deep." Spiritually, this undifferentiated wholeness can also be compared to the innocent state of paradise without any sense of differentiation
of what is right and what is wrong, or any sense of guilt
which makes man run away from God, except that the
latter is expressed in a personalistic drama in the Bible.
Disharmony, broken relationships, and inner conflicts are
the result of the "fall," whereas the differentiated state of
nature is not necessarily so. Men yearn for the restoration of broken relationships and the return to paradise.
The Confucianists look back with nostalgia to the utopian
state of ancient sage-kings of Yao, Shun, Wen, Wu, whom
Mencius and Confucius praised. The Taoists do not see
the undifferentiated wholeness of "One" which the sage
wants to embrace from the retrogressive historical perspective; they seek the wholeness in nature, here and
now. Whether the ideal state of wholeness is here and
now or in the past or in the future, whether it is expressed
in personal relationships or impersonal Tao, the Christians, the Confucianists, and the Taoists have a common
aspiration to achieve wholeness and harmony in one way
or another.

Psychologically, the state of undifferentiated "One" is comparable to the psyche of a newborn baby. One of the characteristics of a newborn child is that he does not make a distinction between "me" and "the rest of the world" in his mental representation. One of the major achievements in human maturation is that of "establish-ing functional boundaries" or "ego boundaries." [44] The function of ego boundary is to "protect the preconscious and conscious ego from intrusions which prove disinte-gration," just as the national boundary is for the protec-tion of national integration. To determine whether a person is healthy and mature is to see whether he has effective ego boundaries in his mental representation. A mature nation cannot allow its boundaries to be undeter-mined. This is also true of a mature person.

Is the state of undifferentiated "One" which the Taoist sage wants to embrace the same as the state of infant nondistinction between "me" and "the rest of the world"? In answer to this question, we may well consider Fung Yu-lan's subtle distinction between "having no-knowledge" and "having-no knowledge." [45] Sagehood is achieved only after one has passed through a prior stage of having knowledge which comes from distinctions, discriminations, and differentiations of things. Sagehood is achieved by transcending the knowledge one has accumulated so much that his knowledge seems nonexist-ent. In contrast, the state of infant ignorance is "having-no knowledge." There have been Taoists who identify the sagehood with the state of infant ignorance, and even propose the return to the primitive simple state of existence. But, in fact, the true sagehood is not the physical simplicity, but the spiritual state of transcending all distinctions, differentiations, and discriminations and the state of seeing things in this phenomenal world from the infinite point of view of the Tao. It is only from the transcendental infinite point of view that one can under-stand the truth of nonduality—"that" is also "this," and "this" is also "that." The undifferentiated wholeness in

Taoist sagehood is the transcendental state of wholeness. It is transcendental and he who transcends does so "in spite of" this or that.

This transcendental attitude was well expressed by Chuang Tzu in his invitation to the state of ecstatic forgetfulness: "Let us forget life. Let us forget the distinction between right and wrong. Let us take our joy in the realm of the infinite and remain there." [46] For the Taoist sage, the problems of how to preserve life and how to avoid harm and danger are no longer problems. He is no longer troubled with worldly gain or loss, good luck or bad luck, victory or defeat, success or failure, in spite of the fact that there are distinctions between gain and loss, between good luck and bad luck, between victory and defeat, and between success and failure. He forgets the distinction between right and wrong in spite of the fact that there is such a distinction. Is this not close to the doing of God, who "makes his sun rise on the evil and on the good, and sends rain on the just and on the unjust" (Matt. 5:45)? Is this not close to what God's grace and impartialities are all about? In spite of the fact that there is a distinction between good and evil, and between the just and the unjust, God still does send his rain on both and makes his sun rise on both. Since the concept of God functionally epitomizes Christian maturity, there is a common emphasis in Christian maturity and Taoist maturity.

Unless we obtain this transcendental point of view, the problem of racial discrimination and other similar problems cannot be solved. In spite of the distinction between East and West, between Jew and Greek, between male and female, we are all one if we can see things from the transcendental point of view. The desegregation brought about by boycott and other means of enforcement is merely a temporary solution of the racial problem. Unless we really achieve this transcendental state of nondiscrimination, nondistinction, and nondifferentiation, there will be endless struggles and conflicts between races, nations, and professions. This transcendental state is essentially that of self-transcendence which is the unique characteristic of human nature. In Confucianism, this transcendence is encouraged, but it is not the basic element in the practice of human-heartedness which is graded according to the nature of relationships. None can supersede the father-son relationship, the virtue of filial piety. Confucianism is this-worldly, and therefore it sees things from the finite point of view. The self-transcendence it encourages is to extend the practice of human-heartedness toward all men under the graded scheme of relationships. The self-transcendence in Gordon W. Allport's "self-objectification" is also this-worldly and from the finite point of view, and there is strong ego-boundary in the mind of the mature self-objectified person and clear distinctions, differentiations, and discriminations in his reality perception in this world. In different ways and various degrees, mature persons are self-transcendent in either psychology, or Christianity, or Confucianism, or Taoism.

This transcendental wholeness is manifested in the empathy and identification of the sage. It can be understood as love. Lao Tzu said:

> The sage has no definite ideas of his own, but regards the people's ideas as his own. I treat the good ones with goodness; and I also treat the bad ones with goodness. Thus, goodness is attained. I treat the honest ones with honesty; and I also treat the dishonest ones with honesty. Thus, honesty is attained.[47]

This may seem to imply that the sage is an uncreative person without his own independent ideas and eager to conform and to identify. But this is not so. In spite of his own uniqueness, self-respect, and integrity, he is well prepared to regard the people's ideas as his own. In spite

of being treated badly and dishonestly, he still treats
others with goodness and honesty. The unique idea of the
sage is his self-transcendence, impartiality, and readiness
to identify with others, because he has achieved the state
of nondistinction, nondiscrimination, and nondifferentiation. It is the state of seeing things in their wholeness,
rather than in their particularities and partialities. This
suggests that analytical knowledge is not enough, because analytical knowledge is concerned with the particularities and the details of things. The Taoist sage favors
the transcendental state of wholeness. Once Nan-Po
Tzu-K'uei asked old Nü-Yü and was told that the one who
had learned the Tao was able to transcend this world and
see the One. "Having seen the One, he was then able to
abolish the distinction of past and present." [48] Then he
was able to enter the realm of neither life nor death. The
Taoist sage transcends not only all distinctions, differentiations, and discriminations of the mundane world but
also time itself.

One may tend to think of the Taoist way of life as
irrelevant, as René Dubos points out in his study of the
concept of health in the history of mankind.[49] It appears
that Taoism was "not designed to solve the difficulties
arising from contacts," and that it offers a kind of
escapism without the spirit of new adventure. There are
these tendencies in Taoism. Chuang Tzu was so otherworldly that he was severely criticized by the Confucianists, though he greatly influenced Chinese landscape
artists and made it easier for Buddhism to be introduced
to China. But Lao Tzu was this-worldly and much
concerned about social reform. He was as firmly convinced of the goodness of human nature as Confucius was
of the possibility of sagehood. His wisdom contributed to
the thought-treasure of the world. Certainly there are so
many evil men who deliberately fail to respect the rights
of others in reacting to nonaction (*wu wei*) that Lao Tzu's
way of life seems remote and irrelevant in this competi-

tive modern world. However, just *because* of the rampant egoism in this "civilized" world, his insight into nature and human relationships appears to be much more needed today than ever.

# VI

# Buddhist Maturity

BUDDHISM was founded by Siddhartha Gautama in India in the sixth century B.C. He was born a prince of the Gotama clan in northern India at the foot of the Himalayas. His mother died seven days after his birth. His father, Suddhodana, the ruler of a tiny kingdom, surrounded him with luxuries. In his early youth, he was unusually sensitive to the enigmas of human existence. He was dissatisfied with sensual pleasures and ambitions of the world; he was troubled with the fact that he too was subject to old age, sickness, sorrow, and death. His family endeavored to distract him completely from these concerns and to insulate him from the signs of human suffering, but without success. At the age of twenty-nine, he made a resolution to seek ways of release from the cycle of rebirth. For six years, he tested and rejected physical asceticism. Finally in a single night of intensive meditation under a tree on the bank of a river he achieved enlightenment and later developed his own unique diagnosis and teachings. He next embarked on a missionary career and formed a community of mendicant disciples from all castes and both sexes. He died at the age of eighty.

Since that time, Buddhism has spread to China, Japan, Korea, and other countries in Southeast Asia. In the course of its historical development, Buddhism has taken three distinctive forms: (1) the fixed, unified, and established Hinayana Buddhism or Theravada Buddhism (Ceylon, Burma, Thailand, Laos, and Cambodia), (2) the diffused and complex Mahayana Buddhism (China, Japan, and Korea), and (3) the esoteric Tantric Buddhism (Tibet, Mongolia, and parts of Siberia). These have divided again into various schools which claim unique or semi-unique interpretations of the Buddhist faith. Like other organized religions of the world, Buddhism is pluralistic and diversified in its religious experience and interpretation. It has to meet the needs of the individual as well as of society in its particular historical setting. Therefore, it is difficult, if not impossible, to make generalizations that would cover all particularities in each school or sect. Today, under the impact of conflicting ideologies and modern science and technology, Buddhism, like other great religions, is undergoing vast internal changes which further prohibit simplified generalizations.

All Buddhists have one thing in common, however. They all have goals and ideals in their religious pilgrimages, although their goals and ideals may be interpreted differently. They are expressed in terms of *nirvana, arhat, bodhi, bodhisattva,* and so on. What are the Buddhists trying to achieve in their strenuous religious disciplines and practices? It seems that what they want to achieve is the resolution of inner conflicts that can be described as the internal integration of personality, and harmony with the ultimate reality. Their goals represent their concept of maturity, though these ideals are expressed in religious terms. They are negativistic, impersonal, mystical, and otherworldly.

In Buddhism, maturity can also be seen both as a process of becoming and as an ideal state toward which the process is moving. When it is seen as a process, "enlightenment" is gradually taking place, as was advocated by the Northern School of Ch'an Buddhism in China (Shen-hsiu). On the other hand, when it is seen as an ideal state, it tends to be understood as what is ultimately real, as seen by the Southern School of Ch'an Buddhism. On the whole, the achievement of Buddhist maturity is a long process which, according to Buddhist beliefs, may require several cycles of rebirth. The term "Western Paradise" has a strong static connotation and implies a final perfect state which is extraterrestrial. Similarly, there is the term *parinirvana* (great nirvana) which describes the condition of the Buddha, when he died at the age of eighty, with a cessation of all existence. This is to differentiate it from the state of enlightenment attained at the age of thirty-five.[1]

The Buddhist frame of reference sees the reality of life as occurring through countless cycles of rebirth which operate according to the law of cause and effect. It also sees the existence of each individual as the striving for liberation from these cycles of rebirth to the state of nirvana. What is this state of nirvana?

### 1. NIRVANA, ENLIGHTENMENT, AND NONDUALITY (INTEGRATION)

What the Buddhists try to achieve is internal integration. The struggle of Buddha in his lifetime can be understood from this perspective. Behind all mythologies about his life story, there was this struggle for the resolution of conflicts within him. His exposure to stark reality created severe conflicts in him and greatly shattered his peace of mind. He could no longer stay in the palace of luxury, pleasure, and material comfort. In his exposure to sickness, death, old age, and hunger, he had been shaken to the ground of his being. He was constantly tormented by the riddle of life. The nature of this torture was inner conflict, and its solution internal integration.

When the Buddha was enlightened, he preached Four Truths: life is suffering; suffering has a cause; suffering can be suppressed; and the way to do this is to follow the

Eightfold Path, namely, right view, right intention, right speech, right action, right livelihood, right effort, right mindfulness, and right concentration. His goal was the cessation of human suffering. Ignorance (*avidya*) is the cause of suffering because man sees the unreal world as real, and craves it. The repeated word "right" in the Eightfold Path means not only "right" morally but "right" in correctly seeing the unreal world as illusion. The Buddha held that the destruction of all desires is essential. Conflicts arise because of man's desires in this world. When desires are destroyed, enemies are conquered and peace is achieved. Surely, "there is no satisfied lust, even by a shower of gold pieces." [2] The enlightened one is wise because he knows that lusts cause pain. Even in the heavenly pleasures, he finds no satisfaction. He who is fully awakened delights only in the destruction of all desires.

Although the Buddha used the conceptual word "ignorance" in describing the fundamental cause of human suffering in his formula of life cycles, the factual cause of human suffering is man's desire, which generates internal conflicts. Victory is well expressed in the Sanskrit word *nirvana,* which etymologically means (1) "blowing out," in the sense of extinguishing the flame of fire, and (2) "blowing out," in the sense of cooling one's passion. In Buddha's Fire-Sermon, nirvana is described as a state in which all flames of greed, lust, and hatred are completely cooled and blown out. Therefore, nirvana implies the total annihilation of worldly desires.

In reading Buddhist literature, one often comes across passages indicating that nirvana is beyond description. The Buddha remained silent when questioned about nirvana. He seemed to take the position that man cannot elucidate what is by its nature incomprehensible, indescribable, and inscrutable. He compared the man who wanted to know what nirvana is to one who was "wounded by a poisoned arrow."

This, however, cannot satisfy the quest of the human

mind. Efforts have been made to describe nirvana. In the dialogue between King Milinda and the Buddhist monk Nagasena,[3] nirvana is compared to lotus, water, medicine, space, and mountain peak. "Just as the lotus is unstained by water, so also is nirvana unstained by all the defilements of the world; just as cool water allays feverish heat, so also nirvana is cool and allays the fever of all the passions; just as water removes the thirst of men and beasts that are exhausted, parched, and overpowered by heat, so also nirvana removes the craving for sensuous enjoyments, the craving for further becoming, the craving for the cessation of becoming; just as medicine protects from the torments of poison and puts an end to sickness and gives security, so also nirvana protects from the torments of poisonous passions, puts an end to all sufferings, and gives security; just as the space is neither born nor grows old, dies, passes away, nor is reborn, so also is nirvana neither born, nor grows old, dies, passes away, nor is reborn; just as the mountain peak is unshakable, so also is nirvana unshakable." The one who reaches nirvana does not cling to pleasures. He is comparable to the water on a lotus leaf and the mustard seed on the point of a needle.

In his attempt to explain what is inexplicable, Kenneth K. S. Ch'en describes it as "a state full of confidence, tranquility, freedom from fear, bliss, happiness, and purity." [4] It is a state of steady, imperishable, eternal beatitude and timeless existence. It is a state that is beyond the world of space and time. It is the infinite transcendent state. It is deep and enduring. The false individuality disappears, while true being remains. From the psychological point of view, Sigmund Freud regards nirvana as "oceanic consciousness of the womb," and Alan W. Watts criticizes it as the confusion of the transcendence of the ego with mere loss of ego-strength.[5] Both are right. "Oceanic consciousness" expresses the nondualistic nature of nirvana which comes from the resolution of inner conflicts, whereas Watts points out its transcendental aspect. The liberation from desires surpasses the ego, rather than falls below the ego.

This nondualistic nature of nirvana becomes even clearer when it is seen from the Mahayana point of view. In Hinayana Buddhism, there are two realms of existence: the phenomenal world is unreal, whereas the nirvanic world is real. The phenomenal world is a conglomeration of elements, whereas the nirvanic world is real because all karmas (deed or act and the consequence arising from that deed) cease and return to elements. But the Mahayana Buddhists are revolutionary in making the nonduality of nirvana even more complete in abolishing the two realms of existence. They insist that if a conglomeration of elements is unreal, the elements that compose it are also unreal. Therefore, it is not only the phenomenal world that is unreal, but the nirvanic world also is unreal, void, and empty. The characteristic of nirvana is nonduality, devoid of all discriminations, particularities, and divisions. This nonduality (integration and harmony) is what "empty" is meant to be. Both the phenomenal world and the nirvanic world are empty. They are not dichotomous. Thus, the phenomenal world also embodies the nirvanic world.

From the Mahayana point of view, the Hinayana's idea of passing from the unreal phenomenal to the real nirvanic world is a delusion. Nirvana is the cessation of all discriminations and dualisms, and the realization that undifferentiated Emptiness is the sole absolute truth. Nirvana is not something beyond this world. Experientially, it is a mental state of transcendental nonduality. In Buddhism, nonduality is expressed negatively as Emptiness and Void, in that both the phenomenal and the nirvanic worlds are unreal. On the contrary, in the Christian doctrine of the incarnation nonduality is expressed positively, in the unity of divine and human nature in one historical person, Jesus of Nazareth. To the

Christian this phenomenal world is real, even though it is transitory. No doubt, the modern youth of the West find it difficult to understand this world-negating Emptiness of Mahayana Buddhism. Their minds are so much oriented toward science and technology, which is analytical, discriminatory, and factual, that Emptiness is a stumbling block to them. From their point of view, to regard the world as unreal is mentally unhealthy. To do so is a distortion of that reality perception which is essential for a mature person. Mental health requires facing reality. Pragmatic functional thinking cannot permit the misunderstanding of the factual world as unreal. To achieve the state of nonduality, nondiscrimination, nondistinction is in a sense destructive because it is a regression to the mental state of a newborn child. This is hard to accept.

The key to understanding Emptiness is transcendence. Enlightenment comes by transcending the ego, the logic, the reason, which is the basis for discrimination and distinction. In the *Heart Sutra*, we read these words concerning the dialectic of Emptiness:

> Form is emptiness and every emptiness is form; emptiness does not differ from form, form does not differ from emptiness; whatever is form, that is emptiness; whatever is emptiness, that is form; the same is true of feelings, perceptions, impulses and consciousness.[6]

Without transcendence from the conventional dichotomy, such nondiscriminatory contradictory statements are absurd. It is by total transcendence of dichotomy that Emptiness is grasped. By transcending the consciousness which separates subject and object, the peaceful calm of Nirvana is obtained. When there is ego-extinction, there is a non-difference of world and Emptiness. This is absurd from the point of view of ordinary logic. Emptiness points to the transcendental reality. It is Beyond. It is the mystical identification of opposites. Its logical parlance is: A is what A is not; or, What A is not, that is

A. The secret of Emptiness is the identification of Yes and No. Emptiness is beyond logic. It is the insight into the Oneness of all. This Oneness is its blissful purity, undefiled, immaculate, unconditional, and complete. Because Emptiness is mental transcendental nonduality, nondiscrimination, and nondistinction, "there is no form, nor feeling, nor perception, nor impulses, nor consciousness; no eye, ear, nose, tongue, body, mind." [7] This transcendental nonduality is close to Chuang Tzu's transcendental identification with the Tao, except that Tao is not implied in Buddhist Emptiness. This is one of the reasons that Buddhism was introduced to the Chinese by way of Taoism. "Wu Wei" was used in translating the Buddhist canon into Chinese, but its positive affirmation of this world transformed Buddhism to meet the needs of the this-worldly-minded Chinese.

Ch'an ("Meditation"—in Japanese, Zen) Buddhism is considered to be the most sinicized form of Buddhism. In this school, the rule that monks should live on alms was disregarded. Its slogan was that one who did not do a day's work should not eat. Ch'an Buddhists cultivated fields or gardens to earn their food. They emphasized meditation but broke away from traditional Buddhist practices and attitudes by their iconoclastic attitude toward Buddhas and bodhisattvas and by their disregard for literature and rituals. Meditation is a kind of intuitive method for discovering Buddha in them that transcends individual differences. This discovery of the Buddha nature in oneself, or rather the discovery of identity between the essential Buddha nature and one's true Self, is the Enlightenment. For Ch'an Buddhists, the ultimate is within oneself. No wonder a Ch'an master said that if one should meet the Buddhas or bodhisattvas, he should kill them. In this respect, Ch'an Buddhism was evidently a product of the ontological stage in the development of mankind.[8] It manifests adolescent autonomy and internalization of authority. The Ch'an Buddhists aim at

Enlightenment, the key idea of which is nonduality, internal integration and harmony.

D. T. Suzuki, a Buddhist philosopher whose writings attract many readers in the West, points out that when one has Enlightenment, all opposites and contradictions are united and harmonized into a consistent organic whole. It is comparable to "leaping over a precipice." Without this "leaping over," there is no Enlightenment. It is "leaping over" all rational conceptualizations, discriminations, and differences. When Enlightenment is achieved, one is in a state in which "knowledge and truth become undifferentiable, objects and spirit form a single unity, and there ceases to be a distinction between experiencer and the experienced." It defies intellectual analysis and conceptualization. No one can explain his experience of Enlightenment coherently and logically, because it is characterized by irrationality, intuitive insight, authoritativeness, affirmation, sense of the beyond, impersonal tone, feeling of exaltation, and momentariness.[9] It is the state that transcends all dualism.

Historically, this nonduality was strongly emphasized by the Southern School of Ch'an Buddhism in China headed by Hui-neng, who regarded dualism as bondage. He interpreted the relationship between meditation (*dhyana*) and wisdom (*prajna*) in nondualistic terms. Originally, meditation was meant to be "the exercise to train oneself in tranquilization," and wisdom, "the power to penetrate into the nature of one's being as well as the truth itself intuited." The question arose as to whether meditation and wisdom are separate and dualistic. The Northern School insisted that meditation was first; and wisdom, second. But the Southern School argued that "dhyana is prajna and prajna is dhyana, and when this relation of identity between the two is not grasped, there will be no emancipation." [10] As long as the dualistic conception of the two remains, there will be no Enlightenment. They saw no dualism between self-nature and wisdom; and for them, self-nature which is self-being is self-seeing; and there is a being besides seeing, which is acting. Acting, seeing, and being are synonymous and interchangeable. The relationship between meditation and wisdom is that of oneness between the lamp and its light. Hui-neng declared: "Dhyana is the body of prajna, and prajna is the use of dhyana. When prajna is taken up, dhyana is prajna; when dhyana is taken up, prajna is in it." [11] In this, nonduality is evident.

Functionally, this nonduality determines and is the basis for the suggestive method of Kung-an (in Japanese, Koan) which means "public case," an official document on the desk implying a sense of critical determination of truth and falsehood. It is meant to assist Ch'an disciples to achieve the Enlightenment. Ch'an methods are often irrational, paradoxical, and seemingly nonsensical. For instance, when a disciple asked: "Whenever there is any question, the mind is confused. What's wrong?" the master answered, "Kill!! Kill!!" [12] This may sound absurd, but the alert mind would soon realize that truth is so mysterious, irrational, and paradoxical that logical answers cannot reveal it. Similarly, when a disciple asked who the Buddha was, Master Tang-Shan answered, "Three pounds of flax." This sounds absurd, but it is one of the most famous Kung-ans. They are used for intuitive grasping of the nonduality which is deeply hidden in the consciousness of man.

Man cannot intellectually analyze the nonduality of the ultimate. If one wishes to do so, he will fall into the "erroneous dualism of self and non-self." What one should do is to live and experience rather than try to analyze. Life is much more than the logic that splits man into subject and object. The Kung-an is not for reasoning, but for bringing the mind to a crisis that leads to intuitive enlightenment, to the Buddha nature within oneself. The Enlightenment is the direct confrontation with this inner reality. The critical state is a kind of psychological impasse that comes into existence when one's reason is at its dead end and one's brain is shattered. This critical state prepares for the Enlightenment, the experience of the nondualistic ultimate reality within oneself. It is the discovery of one's ground of being. The goal of man is to reach this ground. It is here that man attains his highest consciousness. It is here that the ultimate reality unfolds. The one who attains it is the "master of his own." [13] He behaves and acts spontaneously because his life and actions emerge directly from the center of his own being. He draws freely upon his own potentialities. From this point of view, it is understandable that Philip Kapleau interprets *satori* ("Enlightenment") in terms of self-realization.[14] This can be seen as the internal integration of personality or the unification of oneself with the ultimate reality within him.

This ultimate reality is not personal being, as some Westerners may think. The Buddha nature is impersonal. Consequently, it is improper to use the personal term "Self" in expressing the Enlightenment as reconciliation of oneself with the Self. It is akin to the identification with the Tao in Chuang Tzu, but Taoist mysticism is naturalistic, not introverted. The subjective experience of communion and union with the living Christ by Christians is not introverted inner search of the ground of being; rather, it is by nature interpersonal. Confucian self-cultivation is by no means irrational or transcendental. It is always in the context of social environment and interpersonal relationships. It is this-worldly. It affirms discrimination, distinction, and differentiation. Extension of knowledge is essential in Confucian self-cultivation, while Ch'an Enlightenment is beyond reason, intellect, and logic. However, in different ways and forms Ch'an Buddhists achieve their internal integration and harmony, the nonduality of the ultimate, the Emptiness (*sunyata*), the *Nirvana*.

## 2. Love and External Harmony

Man strives to resolve not only his internal conflicts in achieving nonduality but also his external conflicts in achieving harmonious relationships with other human beings and his environment. The Buddhists, however, are more interested in the resolution of the internal conflicts than the external conflicts. Even so, they have had to work out harmonious relationships with the external cosmos at least conceptually and with their social environments in the course of history. The eremitical ideal of the early Buddhist community (*sangha*) was soon modified. The wandering monks began to settle in certain places during particular seasons of the year because of the rains. Instead of begging for alms, monks were happy to accept the generosity of rich patrons. *Vinaya* rules were established for the harmony of the community of monks. In the Pali canon there were more than two hundred rules to regulate the community. In response to the criticism that the Buddhists were turning their wives into widows, their sons and daughters into orphans, impairing normal family and social life, the Buddha made provisions for lay disciples who retain the household life and fulfill functions in society. In order to satisfy the needs of the laity, the multifarious gods in the Indian pantheon were incorporated into their system so that the new converts would feel at home. In some cases, the community of Buddhist monks and the government became identical in search of external harmony with society. In China, this was particularly so during the T'ang dynasty. Sangha became a "state sangha." The ordination certificates of Buddhist monks were given by governmental officials. On the other hand, the external environment does not allow total separation and isolation. Today, the "church and state" issues cannot be avoided whenever there is any established Buddhist community. Even though Buddhism is such a this-world-negating religion, it cannot deny external harmony if it wants to survive institutionally. Today, the neo-Buddhists throughout Asia are struggling with issues about Buddhism and natural sciences, Buddhism and Communism, Buddhism and modernization, and so on.[15] They assert that Buddhist doctrine fully accords with the conclusion of the natural sciences, is in tune with modern cosmology, is a religion of the oppressed, but they are also aware of the danger of losing their unique Buddhist identity and spirituality. Marxists are their allies in their struggle against Western theism. They try to avoid the alternative between Buddhism and Communism.

In Hinayana Buddhism, the ideal goal is to become an arhat, a man who has attained perfection in the threefold discipline of morality, concentration, and wisdom. One becomes an arhat all by himself, for himself, and through himself. Consequently, this ideal is criticized for being too narrow spiritually, too individualistic, and too limited to the elite. This may be comparable to Confucian self-cultivation, but, in fact, arhatship does not have the positive emotional dimension that characterizes psychological maturity, Christian maturity, and Confucian maturity. The Eightfold Path consists of right view, right intention, right speech, right action, right livelihood, right effort, right mindfulness, and right concentration. It is noteworthy that the adjective "right" is used instead of "loving." "Right" is a cold word which appeals to one's sense of conceptual morality rather than to the emotions.

It is not, however, impossible to find the teaching of love in Buddhism, though in Buddhism there is no such overwhelming emphasis on love as there is in Christianity. Virtues, such as loving friendship or loving-kindness (*metta*) and compassion (*karuna*), are emphasized. But the Buddhist makes a distinction between loving friendship and the worldly sense of love (*pema*). The former is altruistic and inclusive, whereas the latter is egoistic and exclusive. *Metta* expresses the proper Buddhist attitude toward others. From the *Metta Sutta*,[16] which is some-what comparable to the thirteenth chapter of First Corinthians in the Bible, we find that loving friendship does not deceive another, nor despise any person whatsoever in any place, nor wish any harm to another out of anger or ill will, but is like a mother protecting her child at the risk of her own life, without any hatred or any enmity. It is to cultivate a boundless heart toward all things, so that the thoughts of boundless love would pervade the whole world, above, below, and across, without any obstruction. It is love without desire to possess others, but to help, to respect the rights of others, and to sacrifice for the well-being of humanity, for all living creatures, not merely for men. It is unlike the Christian agape in its intensity, self-giving, and personal orientation. The mature Buddhist has compassion (*karuna*) and sympathy for the suffering of others both mentally and physically. He has the capacity to rejoice in the success of others without envy or hypocrisy and to identify with others. But this is not the highest value in Buddhism. Fellowship and community are not essential to the Buddhists. The enlightened ones tend to detach from physiosocial contact with others and withdraw from the world. The way to nirvana is a solitary way. If there is fellowship within the community of monks, it is merely on the human level and not the religious. There is no corporate nature of worship in Buddhism, even though they are together for meditation.

Despite the fact that the path to nirvana is a solitary one and the phenomenal world is unreal in Buddhism, among the Pali texts we can find Buddha's guidance to the laity on daily conduct.[17] In five ways the child should minister to his parents: once being supported by parents, he should now be their support, perform duties incumbent on them, keep up the lineage and tradition of his family, and make himself worthy of his tradition. In five ways, the parents who are ministered to by their child should show their love for him: they should restrain him from vice, exhort him to virtues, train him to a profession, contract a suitable marriage for him, and in due time hand over his inheritance. In five ways pupils should minister to their teachers: they should rise from their seats in salutation, wait upon them, learn eagerly, serve personally, and pay attention when they receive their teaching. In five ways teachers who are ministered to by their pupils love their pupils: they should train them in that wherein they themselves have been well trained, make them hold fast to that which is well held, thoroughly instruct them in the lore of every art, speak well of them among friends and companions, and provide for their safety in every quarter. Just as Confucian social teachings begin with the father-son relationships, Buddha started with parent-child relationships and then teacher-pupil relationships. But he ignored the importance of giving guidance concerning sibling relationships which Confucianism considered to be among the five important interpersonal relationships.

However, husband-wife relationships come later in the hierarchy of Buddha's scheme of instruction. In five ways the husband should minister to his wife: he should respect her, be courteous, be faithful, hand over authority to her, and provide her with adornment. In five ways the wife who is ministered to by her husband should love him: she should perform her duties well, be hospitable to the kin of both, be faithful, be watchful over the goods he brings, and be skillful and industrious in discharging all her business.

Then come friendship and master-servant relationships. In five ways the clansman should minister to his friends: he should be generous, be courteous, be benevolent, treat them as he treats himself, and be as good as his word. In five ways his friends who are thus ministered to should love him: they should protect him when he is off his guard, protect his property, become a refuge in danger, not forsake him in trouble, and show consideration for his family. In five ways the master should minister to his servants and employees: he should assign them work according to their strength, supply them with food and wages, tend them in sickness, share with them unusual delicacies, and grant leaves at times. In five ways servants and employees who are thus ministered to should love their master: they should rise before him, lie down to rest after him, be content with what is given to them, do their work well, and spread abroad his praise and good fame.

Finally, instructions were given as to the ways of treating brahmins and recluses. In five ways the clansman should minister to recluses and brahmins as the zenith: he should be affectionate in act and speech and mind, keep open house to them, and supply their temporal needs. In six ways the recluses and brahmins who are ministered to as the zenith show their love for the clansman: they should restrain him from evil, exhort him to good, love him with kindly thoughts, teach him what he has not heard, correct and purify what he has heard, and reveal to him the way to heaven. Likewise, in Confucianism those learned scholars (*shih*) who are often rulers are at the zenith. In all human relationships, loving-kindness is essential. It is the source of harmony.

In Mahayana Buddhism, the ideal goal is the *bodhisattva,* who is destined for the Enlightenment and represents the epitome of compassion, love, and altruism. He is not primarily concerned with his own salvation but does all he can for the salvation of others. He is so compassionate that he is sure to have the "feeling of commiseration" toward the suffering of others. Buddhist compassion is often channeled into establishing hospitals and dispensaries, and the care of the poor and the needy. But it is rather doubtful that there is great concern for personality in Buddhism in terms of warm interpersonal relationships, because, essentially, the Buddha nature is not personal. It is of the nondualistic Emptiness.

Furthermore, Buddhism is extremely individualistic and

subjective. As the leaper should do his own leaping, so too the Ch'an masters cannot do anything unless the disciple has fully prepared himself. The Ch'an Buddhists say, "Unless it grows out of yourself, no knowledge is really of value to you; a borrowed plumage never grows." [18] The social nature and human community is not emphasized, because Buddhism is oriented toward the inner-directed man, rather than the outward-directed man. Enlightenment is the most thorough inner perception. Because it is self-authenticating, it needs no objective validation. In one sense, we can say that there is no reference in Buddhist Enlightenment to interpersonal affective relationships as there is in the interpretation of Christian maturity, psychological maturity, and humanistic Confucian maturity. But in daily conduct Buddhists are bound to have interpersonal relationships, and the master often perceives and closely understands the minds of his disciples.

The Buddhist concern for external integration and harmony is expressed also in their cosmology. Buddhists created interpretations of the cosmos in order to achieve conceptual harmony with the universe. Thus they are able to maintain unity in their thinking. The dichotomous two realms of existence in Hinayana Buddhism were unified by the Mahayana Buddhists who interpreted them both as unreal, void, and empty. It is significant that both Hinayana Buddhism and Mahayana Buddhism were brought to China, but the dichotomous Hinayana Buddhism did not survive there for very long. When Buddhism was introduced to China, it was interpreted in Taoist terms and sinicized. The more this-worldly and naturalistic Ch'an Buddhism emerged. In Ch'an Buddhism, there is a common saying, "In carrying water and in chopping firewood, therein lies the wonderful Tao." Nirvana is not to be sought in another world. It is here and now. This is similar to Chuang Tzu's idea that Tao is even in human excrement and urine.[19] Because of the this-worldly nature of Ch'an Buddhism, which is better known in the West as Zen, it has attracted mystically-minded youth and philosophers in the United States and other Western countries.

The this-worldly nature of Ch'an Buddhism can be illustrated by an ironic episode, which results from the belief that when one is enlightened, he sees the Buddha nature everywhere and in everything. A monk once spat on the image of the Buddha in a temple. When he was accused of blasphemous behavior, he simply said, "Please show me a place where there is no Buddha nature." [20] Since the Buddha nature is inherent in everything and everywhere, there was no place for him to spit. The immanence of the Buddha nature everywhere and in everything in this world may sanctify the phenomenal world and thus enable the Buddhists to live comfortably in it. This may provide them with a religious basis for believing in the harmony of the universe. Yet they are not supposed to be attached to this world.

Among the schools of Chinese Buddhism, T'ien-t'ai and Hua-yen deserve special attention because of their emphasis on the ideas of the harmony of the phenomenal world and the nirvanic world. In the teaching of Chih-i (538–597), the founder of T'ien-t'ai, one can find this universal harmony expressed as "one-in-all" and "all-in-one" (originally from India). Owing to the attainment of concentration and insight, the cycle of life and death is the same as nirvana and nirvana is the same as the cycle of life and death.[21] All possible worlds are much identified and involved with one another.

In expounding the Avatamsaka Sutra (Hua-yeng Ching), Fa-tsang (643–712) became so well known for his powerful exposition that he was invited to the palace of Empress Wu. He pointed out the perfect harmony of the whole universe through interpenetration, mutual identification, inclusion, and implication. He stresses that all things coexist, interweave, interrelate, and mutually reflect. Speciality implies generality, and generality implies speciality. Substance implies function, and function implies substance. When one arises, all arise with it. One implies all, and all implies one. The one and the many establish each other. Only when the one is completely the many can it be called the one; and only when the many is completely the one can it be called the many. In *The Treatise on the Golden Lion*, he expounded how all phenomena are in great profusion, and are interfused one with the other. But they are not fixed. From the transcendental point of view, the all is the one and the one is the all, for both are similar in being unreal. This may remind some of us of the Christian belief in the Holy Trinity—God the Father, God the Son, God the Holy Spirit, Three-in-One and One-in-Three—and that the Christian faith stresses the corporate nature of maturity, the maturity of the Christian community rather than individual maturity, the unity and harmonious relationships among its members.

Briefly, in Buddhism we see how the Easterners strive for internal integration and harmony as well as external integration and harmony in the forms of *arhat, nirvana, sunyata, bodhi, bodhisattva,* and the like.

# VII
## Maturity, Integration and Harmony

THE SEARCH FOR MATURITY is inherent in human life and an inescapable part of man's quest for goals, ideals, values, and meanings. By nature, man seeks to formulate an image of "becoming" in the process of maturation from childhood to adolescence, and from adolescence to adulthood. The formulation of that image is an ongoing process during the entire life-span. Maturity as a state of perfection is unattainable because there is always an "eternal child" within us, as Carl Jung points out. Naïve optimism about human progress toward a utopia has been shattered by the stark reality of human cruelty and destructiveness manifested during the two world wars in this century. We can no longer be misled by the optimism that overestimates the possibilities of "progress" and the consequences of historical change, and that underestimates the difficulty involved.[1] Optimism has been criticized by philosophers, historians, and theologians.[2] The analogy between natural science and historical science, and between natural history and human history, can be false.[3] But the concept of maturity is indispensable because it shows us direction, even though it points to perfection. Pessimism leads only to despair, agony, and death. Without becoming perfectionists, we search for an image of "becoming" as individuals, groups, and nations and set our goals realistically for the future and the present. The purpose of this final chapter is to set forth a concept of maturity and some of its implications.

## 1. THE MATURE PERSON

The process of maturation is the combination of differentiation and integration. This is the underlying principle of human growth. Without differentiation, there is no maturation. Individuality is the result of differentiation. The major task during childhood is to become an individual person. Jung's "individuation," Maslow's "self-actualization," and Allport's "functional autonomy" are concepts describing and expressing the process of becoming an individual and acting as an individual. They have in common the idea of individuality. To be mature is to become an individual and to act as an independent, autonomous, and self-determinative person who is capable of making choices. Erikson's "ego-identity" and "integrity" also have strong individualistic connotations. This individuality is well expressed by Tillich's "courage to be oneself" and the Christian affirmation of faith. It is embodied in the Confucian "ethical individual" through "self-cultivation" in the early phase of Taoism, in the Hinayana arhatship, and in Ch'an (Zen) Enlightenment.

But differentiation needs to be accompanied by integration. From the dynamic, functional point of view, "integrity" signifies the degree of integration. So often, integrity is understood as consistency of values in one's moral behavior in a static sense. If one replaces his old values with unconventional ones, he is considered to have lost his integrity. This understanding of integrity is likely to regard maturity as a state rather than an ongoing process, and make no room for modification or change of values. In this study, integrity is to be seen from the functional and process-oriented point of view, for it means primarily the quality and degree of internal integration in each person. It does not necessarily imply fixed moral judgment. This process-oriented view of integrity is congenial to Freudian harmony between the ego, the superego, and the id in the normal healthy person. It means the unification of one's philosophy of life and the formulation of one's generic attitude. It is the "rectification of mind" in Confucian maturity. Without integrity, there is no individuality in the true sense, for selfhood is divided.

This integration of the individual person is better understood as internal harmony because the word "harmony" does not imply rigidity. A mature person is not rigid, though he is internally integrated around a value system. He is flexible enough to make necessary adjustments to his environment. Although he wants to maintain his identity, which derives from his past experiences, he is capable of accepting new experiences, digesting and absorbing them, and integrating them into a new identity. This capacity for flexibility is the strength of the mature person in his struggle for survival. This flexibility is often manifested in one's freedom, spontaneity, and composure. One accepts himself as he is and respects what he is; he is not at odds with himself; he loves himself in spite of his manifold weaknesses and shortcomings; he upholds his dignity as a human being and is comfortable with himself.

Internal integration is the source of strength whereby a mature person copes with tension and frustration without losing his integrity. One can be calm and serene even though under tremendous external pressures. Without this internal integration, one will be corrupted when confronted with difficulties, hardships, or poverty. It is manifested in one's willpower which is so strong that one can endure the test of deprivation and torture. This is one of the characteristics of the Confucian *chün tzu* (superior man). Tillich's "courage to be oneself" certainly makes this point. He who has the courage to be himself cannot simply be smashed to pieces, even though his physical body endures and is subjected to martyrdom. He has "iron" in his spine.

To become an individual is not enough. Individual

maturity should always be accompanied by social maturity. The mature person loves not only himself but others as well. Loving oneself is identical with loving others. Without loving others, one cannot have genuine self-love. According to Sigmund Freud, human sexuality develops from autosexuality to heterosexuality. Narcissism is self-centered. Therefore, it is a sign of immaturity. As one grows into maturity, he seeks his love objects in others, especially those of the opposite sex. If one's love object is limited to himself, he is certainly immature. The growth of human morality is from heteronomy to autonomy, but the growth of human sexuality is from self-directedness toward other-directedness.

As one grows into maturity, he is released from egoism to sociability. Although Jung's individuation and Maslow's self-actualization have individualistic connotations, both recognize the social aspect of maturity and defend themselves from the criticism of being individualistic. Alfred Adler's individual psychology is also social psychology. The mature person is not tied up with himself, and does not shut himself within his own small shell. As pointed out by Allport, a mature person is characterized by the "extension of the self," which is expressed in one's losing himself for a cause outside himself or in participating in programs for the welfare of others. It is anti-egoism.

The mature person is characterized by his "productive love," the essence of which is care, responsibility, respect, and knowledge. He is ready to give and to receive. A mature Christian is also characterized by his love for others. This love is not to be divided into agape, eros, and philia, for one's love for others includes all three. Any clear-cut distinction among the three kinds of love is false and unrealistic. Tillich's "courage to be" means both "the courage to be oneself" and "the courage to be a part." These two are inseparably interrelated and integrated. Therefore, Christian maturity is not individualistic. It is always in the context of a Christian community, the body of Christ, which is the church. Any quarrel or disunity within the Christian community is a sign of immaturity.

In Confucianism, mature man is filled with human-heartedness (*jen*), and one's self-cultivation is not for his own sake but rather for the harmonization of the world. The mature Confucianist practices human-heartedness and is often in trouble because of his love for others. His maturity is manifested concretely in his interpersonal relationships in the family, the state, and the world. Both the Taoists and the Buddhists are also against egoism and selfish desires. The sage is not self-assertive, nor is he aggressive toward others. He practices nonaction (*wu wei*) because he knows that what matters in interpersonal relationships is one's empathy, love, and respect. He is humble, nonviolent, and meek. In Buddhism, the *bodhisattva*, which is the Mahayana ideal, is the epitome of compassion, love, and altruism, though this love is not expressed in the "I-thou" or "we" kind of interpersonal relationships.

Psychological maturity is concerned mainly with the realms of intrapersonal and interpersonal relationships, reality perception, and the mastery of external environments. But from the Christian, Confucian, Taoist, and even Buddhist points of view, maturity is also concerned with nature, the whole universe, and the Ultimate Reality (God, heaven, Tao, and Buddha nature). It covers both the natural and the transcendental. The mature person is not only integrated within himself and in harmony with other men, but is also in harmony with nature and the Ultimate Reality. He is in a state of self-transcendence which is characterized by unselfishness. He is impartial, all-embracing, and all-inclusive. His outlook is wholesome. He is no longer egoistic, but is liberated and redeemed from the bondage of exclusive individuality. He is open and is one with all things and all men.

But this mature state of wholeness is not the same as

the primeval state or the newborn undifferentiation between "me" and "the rest of the world." It is rather to be
understood as the state of self-transcendence, the state of
"in spite of." If one tries to understand this wholeness
rationally, he tends either to misunderstand it or to find it
incomprehensible, because it contains a paradox at its
center. The Taoists, who identify mature wholeness with
primitive society, are examples of those who try to
understand it from the static point of view. They cannot
understand its true meaning, which takes the form of
unity-in-diversity and diversity-in-unity, One-in-Three
and Three-in-One, One-in-All and All-in-One. They find
uniformity or diversity, totalitarianism or anarchism, and
not the dynamic integration and harmony that takes place
within personality or among personalities.

Mature wholeness neither allows one polarity to dominate the other, nor stresses the "self" at the expense of
the "world." It does not emphasize subjectivity so
strongly that objectivity is ignored. It is the dynamic
integration of the self and the world, the subjective and
the objective. There is no exclusiveness in it. Exclusive
spirituality despises the physical world; exclusive dynamism regards maturity only in terms of process, a process
without direction and destination. Exclusive transcendence is only possible for the otherworldly mystics and
metaphysicians who live in fantasy and illusion—another
sign of immaturity, the characteristic of childhood.

From this study, we can see that the ideal personality
for the mature age of mankind is internally integrated and
externally in harmony with other fellow human beings in
the family, the society, and the world. Independence is
not enough. Interdependence is needed for the mature
age of mankind. The self is not enough, for the world is to
be taken into serious consideration if we are to grow into
maturity. Internal integration needs to be complemented
by external harmony. Self-love needs to go hand in hand
with love for others. Self-respect needs to be expressed in
respect for others.

The source of one's internal integration and external harmony is love, which includes self-love and love for others. Man's basic need is love, to love and to be loved, to receive and to give, to take and to share. Selfhood is born of the mother's love, warm and compassionate, which gives a sense of security and bliss to the child in her arms. Deficiency of motherly love in childhood brings a sense of insecurity and distrust, which in turn hampers personality development. Growth is stunted. Without love, there is no sense of security. Without a sense of security, there is no trust. Without trust, there is no peace of heart. Therefore, without love, there is no internal integration and external harmony. This shows how significant is the formula, "God is love." The mature man is a man of love. A television news reporter said of a churchman: "The Cardinal loved the people and the people loved him. His greatness is as simple as that." On another occasion, a religious leader was eulogized by his former adviser for his unpretentious love manifested in his effort to park a car for an old lady who was having difficulty. These are men of love, and are mature.

On the contrary, the immature man is at odds with himself and does not have peace. Consequently, he becomes dominating, bossy, and tyrannical. He wants to manipulate others and make them feel inferior; he wishes to be honored, and even worshiped as a small god; he always seeks supremacy and the most honored seat. The remedy for this is a change of attitude, without which there is no turning point. Such a change involves the reorganization of the self. But this does not come about by external pressure or by any form of manipulation. It comes when one is loved genuinely and deeply by someone else. With love, the internal wounds are healed and conflicts resolved, and then the disintegrated person becomes whole again. He finds inner peace and external harmony. With inner peace, he is in no need of the emotional support that comes from maintaining racial prejudice, social status, political power, professional prestige, and material wealth. He is no longer like a small child who arrogantly says to his playmate, "My father is *greater* than your father!" Instead, he is humble, spontaneous, and relaxed. His internal integration brings him external harmony.

## 2. THE MATURE NATION

Maturity lies in internal integration and external harmony—the integration of two polarities, the self and the world, the subjective and the objective. When this is applied politically, we can see that the mature nation is autonomous, self-determinative, and independent in its policy-making and administration. It has its own national identity based on its past tradition with its unique cultural heritage and national character. At the same time, it is open to new ideas, new styles of life, skills, and knowledge. It is secure enough to assimilate them into its national life in transforming its character and identity without losing its uniqueness and integrity. It does not become closed and stagnated with old ideas and irrelevant archives. It is not a hermit nation isolated from external reality. It is secure enough to give and take, and the process of internal integration is constantly enforced by this national "metabolism." All sectors of the nation are integrated and harmonious to the maximum degree without losing their respective autonomy and integrity. Its policy is made in accord with reality rather than wishful thinking. Policy makers must have accurate perception into national reality in terms of its economic power, manpower, natural resources, military strength, intellectual power, and spiritual and mental climate. The election of such policy makers depends on the reality perception of the people who cast the votes. Consequently, the nation's reality perception is based on the reality perception of the people as a whole.

Just as the mature person has the strength to sustain

tension, frustration, and hardships, so also the mature nation is capable of coping with external pressures without leading to national disintegration. There are no riots, no internal turmoil. On the contrary, all parties in the nation work together for survival and advancement. The nation collapses if it is too much polarized racially, ethnically, geographically, or culturally. When the nation becomes so fragmented that it disintegrates internally, it loses its strength to withstand external threats. Pluralism and diversity in the nation are a mature sign as long as the nation is able to hold them as unified-pluralism and diversity-in-unity. Then pluralism and diversity increase the nation's strength for combating external attacks. If the nation is split into two or more factions that fight each other, it loses its power. If its minorities are oppressed by subtle discrimination or open manipulation, they are bound to use their creative power for destructive purposes, and thus weaken the nation. The nation becomes schizophrenic. The healthy nation is internally integrated and harmonious.

If the self and the world, the subjective and the objective, are not integrated, one or the other polarity becomes extreme. When this occurs politically, the nation becomes either totalitarian or anarchistic. Totalitarianism is immature because it represents the extreme of the ruler's demand for complete submission of the people and the denial of individual freedom. Anarchism is immature in that it allows each person to go his or her own way in asserting his or her freedom at the expense of other people's freedom. It is immature because it is egoistic on the part of the people. Thus, the ideal state is neither extremely centralized nor extremely localized. It allows integration and harmony between the central and the local, for mature wholeness is expressed in unity-in-diversity and diversity-in-unity. The mature nation is internally integrated and externally in harmony with other nations.

Nationalism is common among nations seeking national independence as in Asia, Africa, and other parts of the Third World. Earlier they were dependent on their colonial masters, oppressed and exploited, but now they are becoming independent, self-assertive, and autonomous. Then they were in their childhood as a nation, but now they have entered adolescence. Their search for independence, identity, and individuality is manifested in nationalism, which often carries an anti-Western flavor. It is comparable to adolescent rebellion against authority figures at home and school. To reach adulthood, it is natural that every nation seeks its unique identity as a people asserting its right for existence as an independent entity with its unique cultural heritage and political structure. Nationalism belongs to the adolescent period of the nation and indicates that the nation is in the process of differentiation and consolidation. To remain in the state of antagonism toward other nations and in isolation from the rest of the world community is immature, unhealthy, and abnormal. The process of integration is needed for its external harmony.

Adolescent maturity is not the final stage of human growth. This is also true of the growth of any nation. National independence should not be the final stage. The independence that is based on national selfhood needs to be integrated with the world in interdependence. The national subjectivity needs to be fused with the national objectivity so that the dichotomy between the two will be resolved. Therefore, nationalism must grow into internationalism because national adolescence should be replaced by national adulthood, and national independence should grow into national interdependence.

A nation can become a nation insofar as it reaches out to other nations in mutual trust, just as a person can be a person only in his relationships with others. The mature nation respects the right and integrity of other nations, just as the mature person respects not only his own right and integrity but also the right and integrity of others. It does not interfere, nor does it manipulate others for its own vested interests. If the nation is not ready to move out into the international scene for mutual dialogue, if the nation is still trying to dominate other nations, it is apparently in a state of inner insecurity and disintegration. It is just like the immature man who tries to dominate because of his inner insecurity and disintegration. It is still setting its house in order like the adolescent boy who shuts himself up for a while until he solves his internal identity problem. A growing nation cannot remain adolescent, just as a growing person must reach adulthood. Once the nation matures and becomes internally integrated, nationalism must go. Nationalism, however, is good and needed for the nation striving for independence and equality in the world community. It has been called the "guiding star of Asian peoples."[4] Once independence and equality have been achieved, nationalism must be condemned, because it blocks the path to the next stage of development in creating the world community, without which there is no peace and national maturity. Once the struggle for autonomy, individuality, and identity is over, the adolescent ceases to be rebellious and resumes his personal relationships with his parents as a responsible adult. When alien forces no longer intrude, and the nation has been reconstituted for a new place of dignity and equality in the world, the nation must turn to positive and creative tasks. This means seeking external harmony with former aggressors who may have caused the rise of nationalism as a consequence of their imperialism.[5] When national adolescence is past, nationalism should be condemned. But patriotism remains, for patriotism is national self-love, which is essential for national maturity.

The mature nation is not the one that dominates the whole world as did the ancient Roman Empire. Rather, it is the nation that is internally integrated and externally in harmony with other nations, no matter how big or small it may be, just as a mature person is one who is internally integrated and externally in harmony with other human beings. The domineering person is not mature, because he is emotionally insecure. The obsessively aggressive nation would be in the same immature stage. During the immature period of human history, the domineering nation might have been regarded as the mature nation because of its childish need for dependence on an almighty father in infancy and early childhood. But this is no longer so during the adulthood of mankind. Just as the independence-seeking nation is half mature in itself, so also is the domineering nation half mature. The dominated nation is immature because it is incapable of maintaining its integrity, for the maturity of a nation is measured by the degree of its internal integration and its external harmony. Mature nations make the mature world possible, just as mature individuals make mature nations possible.

## 3. MATURE RELIGION

An attempt has been made to define "mature religion" based on the analysis of psychological maturity.[6] But this attempt does not deal with religion itself very much. Functionally, the mature religion is the one that is able to provide the spiritual strength with which the individual, society, and the world grow into maturity in attaining internal integration and external harmony, not only through its beliefs but also through its religious practices. It enables its believers to see the world realistically and accurately instead of as an unreal fantasy. Furthermore, it enables them to be autonomous, self-determinative, and comfortable with themselves and to have a sense of identity, integrity, and individuality because of their self-acceptance. Finally, the mature religion enables its believers to cope with the troubles, frustrations, and hardships of life and to be at home in this universe because of their openness and basic harmony with other human beings and with the Ultimate Reality. Basically, mature religion is not narcissistic. Organized religions often lose their vitality and influence as institutions because they have their own egoistic concerns for institutional survival, social prestige, political power, material wealth, and cultural influence. They profess that they are against egoism, but, in fact, they are often guilty of egoism. Their exclusive denominationalism insists that their unique traditions are superior to others. Those who dare to challenge ecclesiastical authorities and differ from the "orthodox" are persecuted in the name of their tribal gods.

In our discussion of "mature religion," we are inclined to ask whether the major religions of the world have grown like a man from childhood through adolescence to adulthood, and to study their developments historically in search of answers. But this is beyond our scope and purpose. Evidently religions do not exist by themselves as independent entities because their birth, development, and expansion depend on their founders and communities of believers. On the whole, it seems that the pattern of development follows that of human growth. It moves from the polarity of the world (external authority) to the polarity of the self (internal authority), and then to the integration and harmony of the two; just as one grows from childish dependence and heteronomy to adolescent independence and autonomy, and then to adult interdependence and mutuality. In early childhood, one's life is full of magical thinking and egoism, but gradually one becomes factual and less egoistic.

The dynamism of human history does not allow stereotyped religious developments following the pattern of human growth. There are regressive times in all developments. In the process of development, there is either differentiation or integration, or stagnation. Even in the

mature stage there are residues from the primitive imma
ture stage. In this modern age, there are still religious
organizations propagating magical supernaturalism for
those who have troubles and are incapable of solving
them scientifically. In some quarters of the Christian
church, there are efforts to make believers constantly
dependent on authority figures, and to represent God as a
magician who works wonders for them in solving their
problems without their own participation. On the other
hand, there are those who heartily echo the proclamation
of the "death of God" and those who identify themselves
with that stream of thought.

The "death of God" may shock or even antagonize
many traditional Christians who are still comfortable
with the religious symbols from the past. In my interviews regular churchgoers said that the first thing they
could think of about God was "Creator" instead of
"Father." They thought of God in the Creation story
rather than the "heavenly Father" revealed in Jesus
Christ. It may be that the "death of God" is a rebellious
self-assertion of man about the termination of childish
dependence on the Almighty Creator for problem-solving.
Modern man is capable of standing on his own feet and of
solving daily problems, and does not need God's help.
Likewise, atheism can be seen from this perspective. It is
man's self-assertion of independence, which is one of the
characteristics of adolescence. The independent man
cannot stand the authoritarian god who acts like a
commander in chief, or a tyrant, or an arbitrary dictator.
Modern man is rebellious just as the adolescent boy must
defy his authoritarian father who oppresses him in his
struggle for autonomy. Mature religion does not advocate childish dependence to enslave its believers. On the
contrary, it encourages their growth into maturity as
self-determinative autonomous persons.

As one grows into maturity, he gradually becomes
aware of the rights of others, gaining in objectivity, and

external integration and harmony. After the hectic years of adolescence, one reaches out to the external world with a sense of identity and to others in equality as a mature autonomous person. He then returns to his father, whom he once criticized, but the nature of his relationship with his father is no longer that of childish dependence or adolescent rebellion, but rather that of mutual love, care, understanding, and responsibility. Likewise, when atheists or the "death of God" thinkers grow into maturity, their adolescent doubt, rebellion, hostility, and uncertainty will give way to receptivity toward the external objective reality, both personal and impersonal, whose ultimate is, it seems to me, what the traditional symbol "God" is meant to be. Adolescent defiance is a temporary phenomenon that is caused by internal psychic needs rather than by external reality. In Christianity, the God whom Jesus Christ has taught is far from being a tyrant, or an oppressor, or a dictator, or a dominator. He is the loving Father. The formula "God is love" should not be offensive to spiritually mature men and women, for the mature relationship is characterized by love. The mature religion is centered on love and justice.

Historically, the Reformers insisted on the right of an individual believer to interpret the Bible for himself in contrast to the prevalent dependence on interpretations by external authorities. This is equivalent to the adolescent assertion of internal authority and the right of becoming an autonomous independent person. If the sixteenth-century Reformation was the product of the process of differentiation in Christianity, the modern ecumenical movement can be regarded as the sign of a new era that is centered on the process of integration. If this is an accurate observation, Christianity is moving toward a stage of maturity. Narrow denominationalism and divisive sectarianism are no longer relevant, though there are those who are still behind the tide of history. But if the present-day ecumenical movement turns out to

be a kind of banding together against defeat, it is certainly
not a sign of maturity. If the modern ecumenical movement is a mature sign, it must embody not only the
process of internal integration but also that of external
harmony. But one should keep in mind that integration
presupposes differentiation. Without differentiation,
there is no integration. If the ecumenical movement
merely represents various churches losing their identity
in one big superchurch, then it is the death of reunion.
Any mature religion is open, inclusive, and all-embracing.

So far, we have discussed mature religion functionally
in relation to its effectiveness in helping the believers to
achieve maturity. But when mature religion is seen in
itself, its maturity depends on its integration and harmony as a religious system. There is no dichotomy in
itself. For instance, the incarnation in Christianity seems
to be the most mature sign because it represents perfect
integration and harmony between the divine and the
human in one historical person, Jesus of Nazareth. It is
the perfect integration and harmony between the sacred
and the profane, the natural and the supernatural. In the
incarnation, God's transcendence is manifested in his
immanence. If the transcendence is not one with the
immanence, it is immature because there is still a dichotomy between the two. The theology that discusses God's
transcendence and immanence in dichotomous terms is
based on the immaturity of human conflicts. The secularization that follows the pattern of the incarnation is a
mature sign of the integration of the sacred and the
profane, the material and the spiritual, the natural and the
supernatural. It would be "less a rejection of Christianity
than a paradoxical offspring of Christianity." [7] If secularization is centered around the polarity of the profane,
then it is as immature as an otherworldly religion that is
centered around the sacred. The mature theological
system holds the tension between law and gospel, love
and righteousness, and integrates the two. Love without

righteousness is not true love, and righteousness without love is not true righteousness, for both are immature and exclusive. If righteousness represents the polarity of the world, love signifies the polarity of the self. But in maturity, the two come together and become so integrated that the loving act is also the righteous act, and the righteous act is also the loving act. The external demand is identical with the internal initiative.

We cannot predict exactly what will happen to world civilization in the future. It seems that mature religion in which men and women can find strength and expression for internal integration and external harmony, individually and collectively, will have a place in it. It is significant that W. E. Hocking foresaw that mature religion in the coming world civilization would be essentially Christian.[8] This may not be agreeable to those who are against Christianity, but its beliefs in the incarnation and the holy Trinity exemplify the principle of integration and harmony.

## 4. MATURE EDUCATION

Like religion, education does not exist as an independent entity. There is no education in the abstract. Without man, there is no education. Though we can talk about educating animals, education in the strict sense exists only for man. Furthermore, educating is done only by man. Although we hear about "teaching machines" of one kind or another, these are designed by teachers as teaching aids or their substitutes. In fact, it is man who makes education different. Consequently, the maturity of the educational system is likely to run parallel to the human maturity behind it.

Some philosophers of education state their positions in terms of perennialism, essentialism, progressivism, and reconstructionism, which represent the fundamental ways men have of making sense of experience education-

ally.[9] Others prefer terms that encourage and support
different kinds of human relationships in education,
namely, authoritarianism, laissez-faire, and democracy.
Each position represents its uniqueness and shares some
common characteristics with others. A comparative
study of different educational philosophies is important,
but our main purpose here is to see them from the point
of view of maturity, integration and harmony. This may
help us see more clearly the kind of education we need for
the mature age that we aspire to reach. At the same time,
we may be helped to see undesirable factors in them that
educate men and women toward immaturity. Functionally, our question here is: What factors in each educational philosophy make us grow into maturity and become internally integrated and externally in harmony
with objective reality, personal or impersonal, ultimate or
penultimate? It must be acknowledged that this attempt
is merely conceptual.

Perennialism is largely a product of Aristotle's rational-
ism and its subsequent treatment by Thomas Aquinas. It
assumes that man's basic characteristic is his ability to
reason, and only through reason can he separate what is
essential from what is accidental and thus come to know
the eternal values and how he is required to live. In
perennialism, the child is helped to rise above nature and
move toward the eternal destiny that awaits him. The
child has free will to reject the truth and the teacher's
authority; however, he must be prepared to accept the
suffering caused by his dismissal of unchangeable and
universal truths. The assumption of perennialism is
internal integration, and its educational objective is external harmony. It aims to make one less egoistic without
violating his integrity, individuality, and autonomy. But
the threat of suffering caused by the rejection of eternal
values and destiny indicates its stress on supernatural
authority over against the internal authority of the
learner. The ideal situation is the acceptance of the

external, supernatural authority by the learner's internal authority, that is, integration and harmony between the subjective and the objective. But when this occurs, it is likely to be the submission of the internal to the external, rather than the coming together of two polarities, the subjective and the objective.

Essentialism, which is also called traditionalism or conservatism, assumes that the values that men must accept are inherent in the universe, waiting to be discovered and understood through natural process or divine revelation. In essentialism, there is a core of essential subjects, certain literary classics, language, religion, mathematics, history, science, etc., that must be learned and stored away for future use. The pupil must accept with confidence the basic experience of past generations and then in turn conserve and transmit this to the next generation. This is authoritarian education, centered on the external authority of subject matter, tradition, and teachers at the expense of the internal authority of the learner. Autonomy, integrity, and individuality are not respected. It certainly makes the pupil less egoistic, but his selfhood may be destroyed. Furthermore, the external harmony does not deal with the present living environment. This makes essentialism less desirable, if it really enslaves us to the past at the expense of the present. Authoritarianism tends to perpetuate childish dependence and heteronomy.

Progressivism, which is also known as liberal education, assumes that in the changing world, man can rely only upon his ability to think straight. In progressivism, the universe is open and man is creative. Therefore, the child must be taught by teachers to be an independent, self-reliant thinker by encouraging him to work at problems he has chosen and defined for himself. While he will have to learn to turn to others for support and encouragement, he must be helped to express what he feels and believes, to discipline himself, and to be responsible for the consequences of his behavior. Above all else, creativity must be supported and sustained. The emphasis of progressivism is on the internal integration of the learner in achieving self-reliance, autonomy, and independence rationally. External harmony with one's environment is not ignored; it acknowledges the necessity of the child's turning to others for support and encouragement; but progressivism is self-centered rather than other-centered. It tends to advocate adolescent maturity because of its overemphasis on the polarity of the self.

Reconstructionism essentially is not very different from progressivism except that it is more impatient and aggressive. It assumes the role of the school as an agent of planned change. In educational practices, the curriculum must choose and teach only the most humane values of the culture for the reconstruction of the social structure. The school is part of the community and must be the kind of place to which people will turn for the satisfaction of some of their needs. The school becomes the place where people work out their value conflicts by understanding one another a little better and by developing common attitudes toward some of their problems. The skills of group discussion make it possible for men to talk over their differences until they come to a consensus, and thus they will have learned how to fulfill their creativity and aspirations. This particular emphasis of reconstructionism is significant because of its respect for other people's equal rights and the harmony of the community. It seeks to achieve internal integration and external harmony. But if the people still hold the adolescent concept of maturity and each cuts the other's throat for his own survival, this goal is hardly reachable even though skills of group discussion are learned by heart. Reconstructionism is based on adult maturity; and it is possible only when people are determined to reach that stage.

Authoritarianism, laissez-faire, and democracy in education are parallel to childish, adolescent, and adult maturity. Authoritarianism assumes that the influences that shape an individual are determined by external forces. Educationally, the teacher is the center of the classroom and demands that the student accept him for what he stands for, his knowledge of facts, judgments of moral values, organization of subject matter, particular framework of instruction, methods and interpretations. How children feel about what they must learn is not important; what is important is determined by the teacher. Thus, children are bound to remain in the state of dependence on external authority and unable to reach adolescent independence, autonomy, and individuality. The external harmony is symbiotic, masochistic-sadistic.

On the contrary, the laissez-faire approach in education assumes that the individual is shaped by internal forces. Educationally, the student is the center of the classroom, and the teacher is more a resource person than a guide, who is ready to help when called upon. Children choose their own subject matter connected to their concerns. So the point to learning is that it satisfies one's immediate purpose; "what he wishes to know" and "when he wishes to know" are the determinative factors in his learning. No doubt, this helps one to become an individual who is independent and autonomous. Internal integration is achieved, but there is no external harmony. The laissez-faire approach in education is centered on the self without any connection with the world; even if there is such a connection, it is oriented to the self.

Somewhere in between is the democratic position, which assumes that an individual is shaped by both internal and external forces, the subjective and the objective. It proposes a completely different human relationship. Educationally, the child chooses from the storehouse of information and subject matter that his elders know and have made of their own experiences, but he organizes it in accord with his needs and problem-solving. He is influenced by the culture, but he in turn learns to shape his culture. He learns to be purposeful by working at his problem in an active way. The teacher is a helper and guide toward material selection and the process of thinking in achieving reasonably satisfactory conclusions. Apparently there is more emphasis on external harmony in the democratic position than in the laissez-faire one. The democratic position tries to help one reach adult maturity, that is, internal integration and external harmony.

Education in every age often reflects on the concept of maturity in its period. If we see education from the perspective of its centrality, it has gone through the period of childhood and also the period of adolescence. One's childhood behavior is determined chiefly by external authority, but gradually this external authority becomes internalized through the process of identification with parents and other authority figures, depending on the intimacy of the relationships one has built with them. The good child is the one who is willing to obey what the parents and teachers say. The good adolescent, however, is the one who is independent and autonomous. The good adult is autonomous and independent, but is aware of the importance of others, thus seeking external harmony. Thus, we can compare the traditional authoritarian education to childish maturity, the liberal progressive education to adolescent maturity, and the democratic reconstructionist education to adult maturity. Authoritarian education is based on the external authority of the teacher; progressive education, on the internal authority of the learner. The former is oriented to the polarity of the world; the latter, to the polarity of the self. But mature education is that which integrates the self and the world, the subjective and the objective. It is based neither on the notion of dependence nor on the notion of independence. It is based on the notion of interdependence. It reflects the nonduality of the process of differentiation and the process of integration.

The recent trend in education is to have the learner participate in the decision-making process in planning the educational program so that his needs can be met. Education has become increasingly individualized. This trend is good so long as it does not go to such extremes that the objective polarity is ignored. If education becomes too individualistic, it will lead to social anarchy. The educational philosophy that is based solely on the polarity of the self is not sound enough, though it is not entirely wrong. So also the educational philosophy that is based on the polarity of the world exclusively is not sound enough. The mature educational philosophy is based on the integration and harmony of the self and the world.

So far, we have discussed mature education from the pragmatic point of view and seen mature education in terms of its effectiveness of helping the child to grow into adult maturity. But there is another aspect of mature education. That is to see the maturity of an educational system in itself. This means that the mature educational system is internally integrated and externally in harmony with objective reality, personal or impersonal, the ultimate or the penultimate. The internal integration of an educational system is manifested in its purposiveness, its unique cultural consciousness, and the integrative series of relationships between various levels and internal working parts within it. It has an order of priorities, which gives direction to the decision-making process. Furthermore, the mature educational system has a harmonious series of relationships with its environment on both the input and the output sides. Educational systems throughout the world today find themselves in crisis not only because of the overpowering rise in demand for more education, acute resource scarcities, and rising costs, but also because of the unsuitability of output and inefficiency.[10] The most serious problem is that the outputs of educational systems are ill-fitted to the rapidly changing needs of the nation and individuals. For the modern world, the educational system must be modernized in its management, its teachers, and the learning process. Furthermore, there should be international cooperation jointly pursuing solutions to common problems. It is significant that in looking ahead, the Working Committee of the Conference on the Ideals of American Freedom and the International Dimensions of Education met some years ago and predicted that problem-solving within and among nations would involve increased planning at various levels and increased international cooperation.[11]

As the history of mankind seems to be moving toward a mature stage, the presently fragmented and mutually isolated disciplines are to be integrated in a cross-fertilization and a multidimensional synthesis for the wholeness of human knowledge. Universities and schools should devote themselves to the search for the whole truth, and not the fragmented, partial truth. The pretensions and excesses of experts should be tamed and they should be subject to the criticism of other disciplines. Knowledge, truth, life, and the world should be seen as a whole.[12] Only multidisciplinary research can be fit to be called the mature science of mankind. This should be the trend. The mature educational system is the one that considers all disciplines to be one, whole and differentiated. But this wholeness does not exclude certain critical distance for the comprehension of its own society, just as the mature person is characterized by self-objectification for realistic perception of oneself. At the same time, this wholeness does not mean uniformity or undifferentiated unity, because the education of man is not animal training. Even if Homo sapiens is everywhere the same and the educational objectives are everywhere the same, the methods of instruction might differ from culture to culture and even from individual to individual. Education is for the whole man and not just a means to a better job or a higher status or national economic development. It is for the reconciliation of all people and all things.

## 5. EAST-WEST ENCOUNTER

"East" and "West" are geographical terms carrying special political, cultural, and religious connotations. They are relative, just as a locality can be a person's east as well as his west depending on where he stands or moves. Within the United States of America, San Francisco and Los Angeles are west, and New York, Philadelphia, and Boston are east. When the standpoint is moved to Europe or Asia, this geographical relation is altered. Similarly, there is no absolute distinction between the East and the West; East and West are as relative as east and west.

To be mature is to meet and to encounter; isolation and exclusion is a temporary adolescent phenomenon of identity crisis in setting one's inner self in order. When the Easterners and the Westerners encounter each other, this relativity of distinction between them becomes clear, and really all men are alike. In facing the tough realities of life, the Chinese were at one time tempted to seek relief through opium and lost their vitality. Eventually they overcame opium. In facing the dehumanization, isolation, and loneliness of the individualized and industrialized society of the West, some young adults find their utopia internally via drugs, Eastern mysticism, and other means of escape. By denying this world, one hopes to find reality in mystical experiences. By taking drugs, one seeks to achieve inner utopia, which is reached by the loss of one's ego-boundaries, a regression to primitive, primary, and illogical thinking. Others seek solutions in communal life or psychologically oriented group sessions. Westerners face the emotional insecurity and loneliness that have made Eastern societies so static and family-oriented.

In the encounter between East and West, each needs to be cautious about the decadent aspects of the other, because fruitful dialogue comes only from the one's careful assimilation of the healthy aspect of the other. The type of mysticism in the East that is apparently harmful to the West needs to be carefully scrutinized. What the West can accept from the East is likely to be its principles of wholeness and harmony, just as the analytical thinking and differentiation of the West is what the East should adopt in the process of growth into maturity. The Hindu nationalist and spiritual leader Mahatma Gandhi made a mistake in refusing modern science and technology in his encounter with the West, because his people needed analytical thinking as much as the Chinese. Blind assimilation of each other leads to further immaturity. Chanting on the street in ecstasy and begging for money in order to support communes will suck away the very life of the Western youth as it has done to the Easterners.

Politically and economically it is commonly held that the East represents communism, whereas the West represents capitalism. Thorough investigation of this stereotyped view is needed, but it is beyond our scope here. Capitalism is characterized by private ownership of property based on freedom of enterprise and freedom of choice by individual consumers, while communism is characterized by the absence of social classes and the ownership of property by the community and not by individuals. In some way, this distinction between East and West reflects Eastern wholeness, nonduality, harmony, and Western differentiation and particularity. But this distinction cannot be pushed too far because each contains some characteristics of the other.

We have seen the "ethical individual" in Confucianism, the individualistic feature in the first phase of Taoism, and the solitary nature of Buddhist Enlightenment. Recently, a distinguished professor of pastoral counseling from the United States spent a year working among overseas Chinese in Southeast Asia. He observed that within the family they were one, but outside the family they were typical individuals. The power struggles within Communist parties indicate the existence of a diversity of views and irreconcilable vested interests among leaders. The existence of dogmatism implies the necessity of repression caused by excessive individualism within the party. The current conflict between the Soviet Union and mainland China indicates the diversity of ideology in spite of Russian effort to have one single center in Moscow for the world Communist movement. The dictatorship of the proletariat, which is in fact the dictatorship of the leaders of the Communist Party, offers an interesting contrast to the individualistic concern that is so clearly stated by Marx in the maxim, "From each according to his abilities, to each according to his needs."

On the other hand, we find social aspects of maturity in psychology, Christianity, and other dimensions of Western society. The West is not only individualistic but also social. It has been pointed out that the traditional notions of the ideal personality in the West are: (1) the rigidly strong character, (2) the self-sacrificing martyr, and (3) the aggressive, independent individual who scorns mutual aid. These traditional notions have now been forsaken.[13] They tend to be oriented to the polarity of the self, but maturity represents the integration and harmony of the self and the world. As one grows into maturity, he finds these notions inadequate. A similar growth can be found in the development of capitalism. In the early days of the industrial revolution, the laissez-faire policy of Adam Smith was adopted in England, but intolerable industrial conditions made necessary the intervention of government for the sake of justice and social harmony. The free enterprise system in reality is not entirely free. It is controlled and regulated, a mixture of private ownership and government control on a prodigious scale. The polarity of the self is not enough. The polarity of the world is needed. All producers adjust their products to the consumer market. The role of individual judgment is significant, but capitalism must be, in certain instances, subject to the government. The differentiated must be integrated, and the independent must become interdependent.

Another stereotyped view is that the East is static, whereas the West is dynamic. This generalization may have to do with the difference in how the ultimate reality has been perceived in the East and the West, and the difference of natural environments. One's concept of maturity often reflects his idea of the ultimate reality that sets his ideals. In Christianity, man is created in the image of God, and man's perfection follows the model of God's perfection. Because the ultimate reality is the living, personal God, those who have faith in him tend to constitute a dynamic society that is not bound merely by laws and order. They have an authority higher than the civil authority. They have the internal authority to direct their action instead of deadly obedience to the external authority. The internalization of the supreme authority made it possible for the early Christian to turn the world upside down. When this dynamism is distorted, it becomes imperialism.

In contrast, the ultimate reality is perceived to be the impersonal Heaven, Tao, and Buddha nature. The impersonal tends to be oriented to nature and inorganic matter. The life experience in the agricultural society is undoubtedly less dramatic and mobile than that in the nomadic society. The plants are not as alive as the sheep and other animals. Consequently, the society that is oriented to nature tends to be static. Chinese society has been built mainly on agriculture. But this generalization cannot be accepted without some reservations. There are some elements of personality in the Decree of Heaven and the offering of sacrifices to Heaven and not offending Heaven. Furthermore, the Tao is described as "Female" and "Infant" in personal symbols. It is significant that human-heartedness (*jen*) was made by Confucius' grandson, Tzu Ssu, to have metaphysical implication with some sense of the ultimate reality. Perhaps this has influenced the Chinese in their interpersonal relationships, that is, in humanitarianism, or vice versa.

Although the ultimate reality is understood as the personal God in Christianity, there are impersonal elements manifested in God's doing.[14] For instance, the God revealed through nature tends to be impersonal, whereas the personal nature of God is fully manifested in Jesus Christ. His love reflects his personal nature, whereas his justice and impartiality reflects his impersonal nature. In human personality, we also find impersonal elements, such as rationality and self-objectification. In our daily experiences, there are times when we are personal, while on other occasions we are impersonal and cold, depending on the dominant aspect of our personality function. But mature personality integrates all aspects of life experiences. Perhaps the personalness of God's being personal is the integration of the impersonal into his personality. This is a paradox, which is the characteristic of maturity. In this paradox East and West are integrated and integrating. The situation may be comparable to the existence of femininity in men and of masculinity in women; in neither man nor woman is the opposite sexuality the dominant factor, yet neither is without it. For the completion of mature adulthood male and female should be united in mutual assimilation and integration without either marriage partner losing integrity.

Whenever external authority is internalized, and wherever there is awakening to the fact that power lies nowhere else but in ourselves, static society becomes dynamic. Submissive slaves would be aware that they too are the makers of history, and old men would continue to create works as long as there is still breath in their bodies. Today, the static East is no longer static. The East as well as the West has entered the period of adolescent awakening. The road toward adult maturity is a long one, but it is the only way by which man can survive. What can we do?

# Notes

Chapter I
A New Era, East and West

1. "Year Out," *Boston Globe,* January 1, 1971.

2. The inaugural address by President John R. Silber of Boston University, 1971.

3. Prof. Jean Mayer's lecture at Phi Beta Kappa, Harvard University, 1971 (*Boston Sunday Globe,* Sept. 19, 1971).

4. Dr. Robert Hamil's sermon at Marsh Chapel, Boston University, Jan. 24, 1971.

5. Patrick Suppes, "Can There Be a Normative Philosophy of Education?" *Philosophy of Education* (Philosophy of Education Society, 1968), p. 12.

6. F. S. C. Northrop, *The Meeting of East and West* (The Macmillan Company, 1946), p. 481.

7. Rollo May, *Psychology and the Human Dilemma* (D. Van Nostrand Company, Inc., 1967), pp. 51–76.

8. Richard E. Dutton, "Science, Cybernation and Human Values," *Journal of Human Relations,* Vol. 17, No. 1 (1969), pp. 77–89.

9. Laura Thompson, *Toward a Science of Mankind* (McGraw-Hill Book Co., Inc., 1961), pp. 227–228.

10. Philip Handler (ed.), *Biology and the Future of Man* (Oxford University Press, 1970), p. 928.

11. W. E. Hocking, *The Coming World Civilization* (Harper & Brothers, 1956), p. 171.

12. Paul Tournier, *The Whole Person in a Broken World* (Harper & Row, Publishers, Inc., 1964), pp. 2–5.

13. Stephen N. Hay, *Asian Ideas of East and West: Tagore*

*and His Critics in Japan, China, and India* (Harvard University Press, 1970), pp. 138–139.

14. "Beautiful, Bright, Rich, . . . and Single," *Boston Evening Globe,* June 20, 1973.

15. Paul Hibbert Clyde, *The Far East: A History of the Impact of the West on Eastern Asia* (Prentice-Hall, Inc., 1958), p. 78.

16. Ichisada Miyazaki, "The Four Periods on the History of Intercourse Between the East and the West," *International Symposium on the History of Eastern and Western Cultural Contacts* (Japanese National Commission of UNESCO, Oct. 28 to Nov. 5, 1957), p. 97.

17. Alice Chase, *Nutrition for Health* (Lancer Books, Inc., 1954), pp. 251–252.

18. Edwin A. Burtt, "Philosophy and Philosophers in the Far East," *Philosophy and Phenomenological Research,* Vol. IV, No. 3 (March 1949), p. 383.

19. Kenneth Scott Latourette, *The American Record in the Far East, 1945–1951* (The Macmillan Company, 1954), p. 137.

20. *The Oxford Dictionary of Quotations,* 2d ed. (Oxford University Press, 1953), p. 294.

21. Géryke Young, *Two Worlds—Not One: Race and Civilization* (London: Ad Hoc Publications, 1969), p. 38.

22. Arthur Christy, *The Asian Legacy and American Life* (The John Day Company, Inc., 1945), p. 231; Cora Du Bois and others, *The East and West Must Meet: A Symposium* (Michigan State University Press, 1959), *passim;* Sidney Lewis Gulick, *The East and the West* (Charles E. Tuttle Co., Inc., 1963), pp. 116–148, 355; William S. Haas, *The Destiny of the Mind: East and West* (London: Faber & Faber, Ltd., 1956), *passim;* S. Hofstra *et al., Eastern and Western World* (The Hague: W. van Hoeve, 1953), pp. 18–22; F. L. K. Hsu, *Clan, Caste, and Club* (D. Van Nostrand Company, Inc., 1963), pp. 1, 192–227; Charles A. Moore (ed.), *Essays in East-West Philosophy* (University of Hawaii Press, 1951), *passim,* and *Philosophy and Culture—East and West* (University of Hawaii Press, 1962), *passim;* C. Northcote Parkinson, *East and West* (Houghton Mifflin Company, 1963), *passim; Orient Occident, News of UNESCO's Major Project on Mutual Appreciation of Eastern and Western Cultural Values,* Vol. VIII, No. 6 (December 1965); Huston Smith, *Accents of the World's Philosophies* (Publica-

tions in the Humanities Number 50 from the Department of Humanities, Massachusetts Institute of Technology, 1961), and "Man's Western Way: An Essay on Reason and the Given" *Philosophy East and West*, Vol. 22, No. 4 (October 1972), pp. 441–459; Géryke Young, *Two Worlds—Not One: Race and Civilization* (London: Ad Hoc Publications, 1969), *passim*.

23. Hendrik Kraemer, *World Cultures and World Religions: The Coming Dialogue* (The Westminster Press, 1961), pp. 15–16.

24. Hocking, *The Coming World Civilization*, p. 51.

Chapter II
Psychological Maturity

1. Carl A. L. Binger, M.D., "Emotional Maturity," in Albert Deutsch and Helen Fishman (eds.), *The Encyclopedia of Mental Health*, Vol. 2 (Franklin Watts, Inc., 1963), p. 533.

2. Carl R. Rogers, *On Becoming a Person* (Houghton Mifflin Company, 1961), pp. 187–192.

3. C. Walton Lillehei, M.D., "Dr. Christiaan Barnard—Some Personal Reflections," *Best Sellers*, Reader's Digest Condensed Books (*Christiaan Barnard: One Life, et al.;* 1971), p. 161. Cf. John P. Bunker, M.D., and John E. Wennberg, M.D., "Operation Rates, Mortality Statistics and the Quality of Life," *New England Journal of Medicine*, Vol. 289, No. 23 (1973), p. 1250; Francis D. Moore, M.D., "Social Investment and Patient Welfare in Organ Transplantation," in Preston N. Williams, George P. Fulton, and Walter G. Muelder (eds.), *Ethical Issues in Biology and Medicine*, Proceedings of a Symposium on The Identity and Dignity of Man sponsored by Boston University and American Association for the Advancement of Science (Schenkman Publishing Co., Inc., 1972), p. 64.

4. David L. Sills (ed.), *International Encyclopedia of the Social Sciences* (The Macmillan Company, 1968), p. 332.

5. Marie Jahoda, *Current Concepts of Positive Mental Health* (Basic Books, Inc., 1958), p. 23. The six categories are: (1) the attitudes of an individual toward his own self, (2) the individual's manner and degree of growth, development, or self-actualization, (3) integration, (4) autonomy, (5) the adequacy of an individual's perception of reality, and (6) environmental mastery. Also see Don S. Browning, *Generative Man:*

*Psychoanalytic Perspectives* (The Westminster Press, 1973), *passim.* Also cf. Douglas H. Heath, *Explorations of Maturity* (Appleton-Century-Crofts, 1965), *passim,* particularly Ch. 1; Robert W. White, *Lives in Progress* (Henry Holt & Company, Inc., 1952), pp. 374–405.

6. Carl G. Jung, *The Development of Personality,* in Sir Herbert Read *et al.* (eds.), *Collected Works,* Vol. 17, tr. by R. F. C. Hull (Pantheon Books, 1953), p. 190.

7. A comment by H. G. Bayness, translator of Jung's works, in Carl G. Jung, *Psychological Types* (Pantheon Books, 1953), p. viii.

8. Erik H. Erikson, *Identity and the Life Cycle* (International Universities Press, Inc., 1959), p. 120.

9. Karen Horney, M.D., *The Neurotic Personality of Our Time* (W. W. Norton & Company, Inc., 1937), pp. 41–59.

10. Jacob A. Arlow and Charles Brenner, *Psychoanalytic Concepts and the Structural Theory* (International Universities Press, Inc., 1964), p. 81.

11. Lewis J. Sherrill, *The Struggle of the Soul* (The Macmillan Company, 1961), pp. 100–128.

12. Gordon W. Allport, *The Person in Psychology* (Beacon Press, Inc., 1968), p. 129.

13. Gordon W. Allport, *Personality: A Psychological Interpretation* (Henry Holt & Company, Inc., 1937), p. 219.

14. F. Barron, *Personality Soundness in University Graduate Students,* Publications of Personnel Assessment Research No. 1, being quoted in Gordon W. Allport, "Personality: Normal and Abnormal" in Hung-min Chiang and Abraham H. Maslow (eds.), *The Healthy Personality* (Van Nostrand-Reinhold Company, 1969), p. 7.

15. Rollo May, *Man's Search for Himself* (W. W. Norton & Company, Inc., 1953), p. 176.

16. Abraham H. Maslow, *Toward a Psychology of Being* (D. Van Nostrand Company, Inc., 1962), *passim.*

17. Erich Fromm, *Man for Himself* (Rinehart & Company, Inc., 1947), pp. 72–73.

18. Allport, *Personality,* pp. 222–224.

19. Erik H. Erikson, *Childhood and Society* (W. W. Norton & Company, Inc., 1950), p. 229.

20. David P. Ausubel, *Ego Development and the Personality Disorders* (Grune & Stratton, Inc., 1952), pp. 57–59, 61; Sigmund

Freud, *Three Essays on Sexuality and Other Works* (Basic Books, Inc., 1962), p. 233; Leon J. Saul, *Emotional Maturity* (J. B. Lippincott Company, 1960), p. 10.

21. Alfred Adler, *The Science of Living* (Greenberg, Publisher, 1929), p. 263.

22. Abraham H. Maslow, *Motivation and Personality* (Harper & Brothers, 1954), p. 342.

23. Harry A. Overstreet, *The Mature Mind* (W. W. Norton & Company, Inc., 1949), p. 63.

24. Jahoda, *Current Concepts of Positive Mental Health,* p. 23; Allport, *Personality,* p. 213.

Chapter III
Christian Maturity

1. Reinhold Niebuhr, *Man's Nature and His Communities* (Charles Scribner's Sons, 1965), p. 109.

2. For better understanding of the two types of religious patterns "intrinsic" and "extrinsic," see Allport, *The Person in Psychology,* pp. 148–151.

3. Paul Tillich, *Dynamics of Faith* (Harper & Brothers, 1956), p. 108.

4. *The Interpreter's Dictionary of the Bible,* Vol. 2 (Abingdon Press, 1962), p. 718.

5. These words are used by the apostle Paul in describing himself (II Cor. 4:8–9). Also see I Cor. 4:11; II Cor. 11:23–27.

6. Paul Tillich, *The Courage to Be* (Yale University Press, 1952), *passim.*

7. Karl Barth, *Church Dogmatics,* Vol. IV, Part 1 (Edinburgh: T. & T. Clark, 1961), p. 101.

8. W. E. Vine, *An Expository Dictionary of New Testament Words,* Vol. III (London: Oliphants, Ltd., 1941), p. 170.

9. Paul Johannes Du Plessis, *The Idea of Perfection in the New Testament* (Kampen, Holland: J. H. Kok), p. 242.

10. Ernest White, *The Christian Life and the Unconscious* (Harper & Brothers, 1955), p. 51.

11. Emil Brunner, *Dogmatics,* Vol. III (The Westminster Press, 1962), p. 299.

12. Reinhold Niebuhr, *The Nature and Destiny of Man,* Vol. 2 (Charles Scribner's Sons, 1951), p. 69.

13. *Ibid.*, p. 290.

14. Paul Tillich, *Systematic Theology,* Vol. III (The University of Chicago Press, 1963), pp. 232–237.

15. Tillich, *The Courage to Be,* pp. 87–88.

16. *The Interpreter's Bible,* Vol. 10 (Abingdon-Cokesbury Press, 1953), p. 629.

17. Paul Henry, *Saint Augustine on Personality* (The Macmillan Company, 1960), p. 25.

18. Peter A. Bertocci, "Three Visions of Perfection and Human Freedom," *Psychologia,* Vol. V, No. 2 (June 1962).

19. Barth, *Church Dogmatics,* Vol. IV, Part 2, p. 499.

20. Sherrill, *The Struggle of the Soul,* pp. 72–128.

21. Cornelis A. van Peursen, "Man and Reality—The History of Human Thought," *Student World,* Vol. LVI, No. 1 (Geneva: World Student Christian Federation, 1963), pp. 13–21.

22. Harvey G. Cox, Jr., *The Secular City* (The Macmillan Company, 1965), pp. 1–32.

23. Karl Barth, *The Humanity of God* (John Knox Press, 1960), p. 46.

Chapter IV
Confucian Maturity

1. Arthur F. Wright (ed.), *Confucianism and Chinese Civilization* (Atheneum Publishers, 1964), p. 5.

2. Wu-chi Liu, *Confucius, His Life and Time* (Philosophical Library, Inc., 1955), p. 155.

3. *The Great Learning,* ch. 5.

4. *Ibid.*

5. Lin Yu-t'ang (ed. and tr.), *The Wisdom of Confucius* (Modern Library, Inc., 1938), pp. 190–191.

6. *The Analects,* chs. 49 and 55. (Originally, "superior man" refers to the ruling class, and "inferior man" to the common people. But Confucius added new meanings to these terms.)

7. Fung's interpretation is based on the text in *The Analects,* 20:3 "Not to know *li* (propriety) is to have no means of standing." See Fung Yu-lan, *A Short History of Chinese Philosophy* (The Free Press, 1948), p. 46.

8. Lin Yu-t'ang, *The Wisdom of Confucius,* p. 123.

9. *The Analects,* 14:41.

10. *Ibid.*, 2:4.

11. Leo Sherley-Price, *Confucius and Christ* (London: Dacre Press Book, A. & C. Black, Ltd., 1951), pp. 51–53.

12. Wing-tsit Chan, *A Source Book in Chinese Philosophy* (Princeton University Press, 1963), p. 3.

13. *The Analects*, 20:2.

14. *Ibid.*, 7:36.

15. Derk Bodde, "Harmony and Conflict in Chinese Philosophy," in Arthur F. Wright (ed.), *Studies in Chinese Thought* (The University of Chicago Press, 1967), p. 63.

16. Wu-chi Liu, *Confucius, His Life and Time*, p. 99.

17. *The Book of Mencius*, 3B:2. For a new translation, see W. A. C. H. Bobson (tr.), *The Book of Mencius* (Toronto: University of Toronto Press, 1963), pp. 124–125.

18. *The Book of Mencius*, 6B:15.

19. *The Analects*, 12:22.

20. Lin Yu-t'ang, *The Wisdom of Confucius*, p. 181.

21. *The Analects*, 6:28.

22. *Ibid.*, 1:3. Also see James Legge, *The Religions of China* (London: Hodder & Stoughton, Ltd., 1880), pp. 261–262.

23. *The Analects*, 7:29.

24. *Ibid.*, 1:2.

25. *The Great Learning*, ch. 5.

26. *The Book of Mencius*, 6A:11; 4B:28.

27. *Ibid.*, 2A:6.

28. *Ibid.*, 7A:45.

29. Arthur Waley, *Three Ways of Thought in Ancient China* (London: George Allen & Unwin, Ltd., 1939), p. 115.

30. *The Book of Mencius*, 2A:3.

31. *Ibid.*, 1A:7.

32. Wei-ming Tu, "The Creative Tension Between *Jen* and *Li*," in *Philosophy East and West*, Vol. 18, No. 2 (1968), p. 38.

33. Richard Wilhelm, *Confucius and Confucianism* (Harcourt, Brace and Company, Inc., 1931), p. 143.

34. Timothy T'ien-ming Lin, "The Confucian Concept of *Jen* and the Christian Concept of Love," *Ching Feng, Quarterly Notes on Christianity and Chinese Religion and Culture*, Vol. XV, No. 3 (1972), p. 170.

35. *The Analects*, 12:11.

36. *The Book of Mencius*, 3A:4.

37. Legge, *The Religions of China,* p. 86.
38. *The Book of Mencius,* 7:9.


Chapter V
Taoist Maturity

1. Wing-tsit Chan, *The Way of Lao Tzu* (The Bobbs-Merrill Company, Inc., 1963), p. 29.
2. Chi-chün Chang, *Lao Tzu* (Taipei: The Commercial Press, 1958), p. 46.
3. *The Analects,* 14:39, 41.
4. Fung Yu-lan, *A Short History of Chinese Philosophy,* p. 62.
5. There are about seven hundred commentaries and more than forty versions in English alone.
6. *The Analects,* 14:41.
7. C. Y. Chang, *Creativity and Taoism: A Study of Chinese Philosophy, Art and Poetry* (The Julian Press, Inc., 1963), p. 77.
8. *Lao Tzu,* ch. 3.
9. *Ibid.,* ch. 19.
10. *Ibid.,* ch. 49.
11. *Ibid.,* chs. 46, 76.
12. *Ibid.,* ch. 64.
13. *Ibid.,* ch. 3.
14. *Ibid.,* ch. 17.
15. *Ibid.,* ch. 8.
16. *Ibid.,* chs. 34, 57, 66.
17. *The Book of Mencius,* 7A:26.
18. *Lao Tzu,* ch. 49.
19. *Ibid.,* ch. 19.
20. *Ibid.,* ch. 71.
21. *Ibid.,* ch. 20.
22. *Ibid.,* ch. 1.
23. *Ibid.,* chs. 25, 34, 35.
24. *Ibid.,* ch. 23.
25. *Ibid.,* ch. 40.
26. *Ibid.,* ch. 41.
27. *Ibid.,* ch. 58.
28. *Ibid.,* ch. 66.
29. Holmes Welch, *The Parting of the Way* (Beacon Press Inc., 1957), p. 23.

30. Lao Tzu, *Tao Teh King*, tr. by Archie J. Bahm (Frederick Ungar Publishing Company, 1961), p. 71; Lin Tu-t'ang, *The Wisdom of Lao Tse* (Modern Library, Inc., 1948), p. 14.

31. Joseph Needham, *Science and Civilisation in China*, Vol. 2 (London: Cambridge University Press, 1956), p. 71.

32. In this regard, it is noteworthy that there is a counter-cultural trend among the young people and the intellectuals in the United States. For instance, in an interview a philosophy professor expressed his particular joy in the fact that their daughter delivered her first child at home instead of at the hospital.

33. H. G. Creel, *Chinese Thought from Confucius to Mao Tse-Tung* (The University of Chicago Press, 1953), p. 103.

34. Ronald W. Clark, *Einstein: The Life and Times* (The World Publishing Company, 1971), pp. 95, 192.

35. *Lao Tzu*, ch. 55.

36. Hu Shih, *Chung-Ku Che-Hsüeh Shih Ta-Kang* (Outlines of the History of Chinese Philosophy), p. 50.

37. *Lao Tzu*, ch. 38.

38. Lewis J. Sherrill, *The Gift of Power* (The Macmillan Company, 1955), pp. 9–14.

39. *Chuang Tzu*, ch. 18.

40. *Ibid.*, ch. 8.

41. *Ibid.*, ch. 18.

42. *Ibid.*, ch. 1.

43. *Lao Tzu*, ch. 22.

44. Norman Cameron, *Personality Development and Psychopathology* (Houghton Mifflin Company, 1963), pp. 13, 227. Also see Joseph Stone and Joseph Church, *Childhood and Adolescence* (Random House, Inc., 1957), p. 85.

45. Fung Yu-lan, *A Short History of Chinese Philosophy*, p. 116.

46. *Ibid.*, p. 114.

47. *Lao Tzu*, ch. 49.

48. *Chuang Tzu*, ch. 6.

49. René Dubos, *Mirage of Health* (Harper & Brothers, 1959), p. 216.

Chapter VI
Buddhist Maturity

1. Kenneth K. S. Ch'en, *Buddhism* (Barron's Educational Series, Inc., 1968), p. 57. Also see G. F. Allen (ed. and tr.), *The Buddha's Philosophy* (London: George Allen & Unwin, Ltd., 1959), pp. 34–35.

2. F. Max Müller (tr.), *Sacred Books of the East*, Vol. X (first published by Oxford University Press, 1881), pp. 49–51.

3. The text of *The Questions of Milinda* (originally in Pali) is in the form of a dialogue between King Milinda and the Buddhist monk Nagasena who answers all the questions being put to him. It is held in high authority.

4. Ch'en, *Buddhism*, p. 58.

5. Alan W. Watts, *Psychotherapy East and West* (Pantheon Books, 1961), p. 31.

6. Edward Conze (ed. and tr.), *Buddhist Wisdom Books—The Diamond Sutra and the Heart Sutra* (London: George Allen & Unwin, Ltd., 1958), p. 81.

7. *Ibid.*, p. 89.

8. See Chapter III, Section 3, "Secularization, Integration and Harmony," pp. 66–71.

9. D. T. Suzuki, *Zen Buddhism*, ed. by William Barrett (Doubleday & Company, Inc., 1956), pp. 84, 103–108.

10. *Ibid.*, p. 167.

11. *Ibid.*, p. 178. Also see Hui-neng, *The Platform Scriptures* (Tan-Ching), tr. with an introduction and notes by Wing-tsit Chan (St. John's University Press, 1963), pp. 45, 49; *The Platform Sutra of the Sixth Patriarch*, the text of the Tung-Huang Manuscript with translation, introduction, and notes by Philip B. Yampolsky (Columbia University Press, 1967), p. 135.

12. *Ts'ao-Shan Pen-Chi Ch'an Shih Yü-Lu* (Recorded Conversations of Ch'an Master Pen-Chi), 840–901.

13. Chang Chung-Yuan, *Original Teachings of Cha'n Buddhism* (Pantheon Books, 1969), p. xi.

14. Philip Kapleau (ed.), *The Three Pillars of Zen* (Beacon Press, Inc., 1965), p. 3.

15. Ernst Benz, *Buddhism or Communism: Which Holds the Future of Asia?* tr. by Richard and Clara Winston (Doubleday & Company, Inc., 1965), *passim*.

16. Winston L. King, *Buddhism and Christianity* (The Westminster Press, 1962), p. 72.

17. Richard A. Gard (ed.), *Buddhism* (George Braziller, Inc., 1961), pp. 222–224.

18. Suzuki, *Zen Buddhism,* p. 97.

19. Chuang Tzu, ch. 22.

20. Fung Yu-lan, *A Short History of Chinese Philosophy,* p. 263–264.

21. Wing-tsit Chan, *A Source Book in Chinese Philosophy,* . 405.

Chapter VII
Maturity, Integration and Harmony

1. Robert L. Heilbroner, *The Future as History* (Harper & Brothers, 1960), pp. 72, 74, 197.

2. Charles Frankel, *The Case for Modern Man* (Beacon Press, Inc., 1956), p. 5.

3. Geoffrey Barraclough, *History in a Changing World* (University of Oklahoma Press, 1956), p. 226.

4. Philip W. Thayer and William T. Phillips (eds.), *Nationalism and Progress in Free Asia* (The Johns Hopkins Press, 1956), p. 71–82.

5. Rupert Emerson, *From Empire to Nation: The Rise to Self-Assertion of Asian and African Peoples* (Harvard University Press, 1960). The central theme of the book is that the rise of nationalism among non-European peoples was a consequence of the imperial spread of Western European civilization over the face of the earth.

6. Orlo Strunk, Jr., *Mature Religion: A Psychological Study* (Abingdon Press, 1965). Prof. James W. Fowler III of Harvard Divinity School has been engaged in a research project on faith development which has great relevance to religious maturity and mature religion.

7. Hocking, *The Coming World Civilization,* p. xi.

8. *Ibid.,* p. 159.

9. A. Perennialism is also called Classicism, Neo-Classicism, Scholasticism, Neo-Scholasticism, Neo-Thomism, and Supernaturalism. Some of the leaders are: (1) secular—Robert M. Hutchins, Stringfellow Barr, Scott Buchanan, Richard Weaver,

John U. Nef, Mark Van Doren, Robert Ulich; (2) Roman Catholic—William F. Cunningham, Jacques Maritain, John D Redden, Francis A. Ryan.

B. Essentialism is also called Conservatism and Traditionalism. Chief spokesmen have been: William C. Bagley William W. Brickman, H. H. Horne, and Isaac L. Kandel.

C. Progressivism is also called Modernism and Pragmatism. Chief spokesmen have been: John Dewey, William H Kilpatrick, Boyd H. Bode, John L. Childs, L. Thomas Hopkins George S. Counts, and Harold Rugg.

D. Reconstructionism is also called Modern Utopianism Chief spokesmen have been Theodore Brameld and John Dewey (in portions of his writings), but have drawn upon others, such as Lewis Mumford, Thomas Mann, G. B. Shaw, H. G. Wells, Kar Mannheim, Harold J. Laski, and Thorstein Veblen.

See Theodore B. H. Brameld, *Patterns of Educationa Philosophy: A Democratic Interpretation* (World Book Company, 1950), and *Philosophies of Education in Cultural Perspective* (The Dryden Press, Inc., 1955). Also see "Minister a Educator—Philosophies of Education," unpublished paper b Prof. Walter L. Holcomb, Boston University (1967), pp. 1–2.

10. Philip H. Coombs, *The World Educational Crisis* (Oxfor University Press, 1968), pp. 166–171.

11. U.S. Department of Health, Education, and Welfare Offic of Education, *Education for Freedom and World Understand ing, a Report of the Working Committee of the Conference o the Ideals of American Freedom and the International Dimen sions of Education,* March 26–28, 1962, Washington, D.C., p. 24

12. Robert M. Hutchins, *Learning Society* (The New Amer can Library of World Literature, Inc., 1968), p. 135.

13. Laura Thompson, *Toward a Science of Mankin* (McGraw-Hill Book Co., Inc., 1961), pp. 227–228.

14. Dean Krister Stendahl of Harvard Divinity School hap pens to consider that the strongest point in God's impersonalit is the Holy Spirit in Acts, ch. 2, which appears to be a impersonal power.

## DATE DUE

| | | | |
|---|---|---|---|
| OCT 3 0 '79 | | | |
| NOV 4 '80 | | | |
| NOV 1 4 '80 | | | |
| OCT 2 6 '82 | | | |
| NOV 7 '83 | | | |
| NOV 2 1 '83 | | | |
| SEP 1 3 '89 | | | |
| FE 2'94 | | | |
| AP 1 2 '95 | | | |
| | | | |
| | | | |
| | | | |
| | | | |
| | | | |
| | | | |
| | | | |

DEMCO 38-297